P9-DUJ-712

6. Enter your class ID code to join a class.

IF YOU HAVE A CLASS CODE FROM YOUR TEACHER

a. Enter your class code and click [Next]

b. Once you have joined a class, you will be able to use the Discussion Board and Email tools.

c. To enter this code later, choose **Join a Class**.

IF YOU DO NOT HAVE A CLASS CODE

a. If you do not have a class ID code, click [Skip]

b. You do not need a class ID code to use *iQ Online*.

c. To enter this code later, choose **Join a Class**.

7. Review registration information and click Log In. Then choose your book. Click **Activities** to begin using *iQ Online*.

IMPORTANT

- After you register, the next time you want to use *iQ Online*, go to www.iQOnlinePractice.com and log in with your email address and password.
- The online content can be used for 12 months from the date you register.
- For help, please contact customer service: eltsupport@oup.com.

WHAT IS iQ ONLINE ?

All new activities provide essential skills **practice** and support.

Vocabulary and Grammar **games** immerse you in the language and provide even more practice.

Authentic, engaging **videos** generate new ideas and opinions on the Unit Question.

Go to the Media Center to download or stream all **student book audio**.

Use the **Discussion Board** to discuss the Unit Question and more.

Email encourages communication with your teacher and classmates.

Automatic grading gives immediate feedback and tracks progress.

Progress Reports show what you have mastered and where you still need more practice.

198 Madison Avenue
New York, NY 10016 USA

Great Clarendon Street, Oxford, OX2 6DP, United Kingdom

Oxford University Press is a department of the University of Oxford.
It furthers the University's objective of excellence in research, scholarship,
and education by publishing worldwide. Oxford is a registered trade
mark of Oxford University Press in the UK and in certain other countries.

Director, ELT New York: Laura Pearson
Head of Adult, ELT New York: Stephanie Karras
Publisher: Sharon Sargent
Managing Editor: Mariel DeKranis
Development Editor: Eric Zuarino
Executive Art and Design Manager: Maj-Britt Hagsted
Design Project Manager: Debbie Lofaso
Content Production Manager: Julie Armstrong
Senior Production Artist: Elissa Santos
Image Manager: Trisha Masterson
Image Editor: Liaht Ziskind
Production Coordinator: Brad Tucker

ISBN: 978 0 19 481838 4 Student Book 1 with iQ Online pack
ISBN: 978 0 19 481839 1 Student Book 1 as pack component
ISBN: 978 0 19 481802 5 iQ Online student website

Printed in China
This book is printed on paper from certified and well-managed sources.

ACKNOWLEDGEMENTS

Illustrations by: p. 26 5W Infographics; p. 83 5W Infographics; p. 148 Barb
Bastian; p. 152 Karen Minot; p. 174 5W Infographics.

*We would also like to thank the following for permission to reproduce the following
photographs*: Cover: Yongyut Kumsri/Shutterstock; Inside back cover:
lvcandy/Getty Images, Bloom Design/shutterstock; Video Vocabulary
(used throughout the book): Oleksiy Mark / Shutterstock; p. 2/3 Hero
Images/Hero Images/Corbi/Corbis UK Ltd.; p. 4 Daniel Acker/Bloomberg/
Getty Images (electronics); p. 4 R Carner/Shutterstock (truck); p. 4 Mike
Goldwater/Alamy (baby); p. 4 Cultura RM/Alamy (construction);
p. 4 Photodisc/Oxford University Press (chef); p. 4 Kinga/Shutterstock
(office); p. 7 Blend Images/Alamy (construction); p. 7 Science Photo
Library/Oxford University Press (doctor); p. 7 Blend Images/Alamy (nurse);
p. 7 Tetra Images/Oxford University Press (chef); p. 7 OJO Images Ltd/
Alamy (accountant); p. 7 Stockbyte/Oxford University Press (lawyer);
p. 8 Tom Wang/Alamy (farmer); p. 8 Image Source/Alamy (gym); p. 8 Serge
Kozak/Corbis UK Ltd. (science); p. 8 Image Source/Getty Images (bank);
p. 8 Image Source/Oxford University Press (designer); p. 8 Echo/Getty
Images (salesperson); p. 11 Wavebreak Media ltd/Alamy; p. 12 OJO Images
Ltd/Alamy (business woman); p. 12 Image Source/Alamy (salesman);
p. 12 wavebreakmedia/Shutterstock (designer); p. 24 John Harper/Corbis
UK Ltd.; p. 25 Peter Dazeley/Getty Images (passport); p. 25 Bettmann/
Corbis UK Ltd. (old photo); p. 25 f-f-f-f/Shutterstock (frame); p. 28 Justin
Kase zninez/Alamy; p. 29 Alex Segre/Alamy (vegetables); p. 29 Paul Brown/
Alamy (festival); p. 31 Tips Images / Tips Italia Srl a socio unico/Alamy;
p. 33 Digital Vision/Oxford University Press; p. 34 John Slater/Stone/Getty
Images (Sun Yun Wing); p. 34 Fotoluminate LLC/Shutterstock (Basher);
p. 35 Jeff Greenberg/Alamy; p. 46/47 Prisma/Superstock Inc.; p. 48 Jill
Chen/Shutterstock (beach); p. 48 Larry Lilac/Oxford University Press
(wall); p. 48 Hero Images Inc./Alamy (mountains); p. 48 Joe McBride/Getty
Images (rollercoaster); p. 49 Paul Heinrich/Alamy; p. 58 Compassionate
Eye Foundation/Steve Smith/Getty Images; p. 60 Gareth Boden/Oxford
University Press; p. 65 Jeff Greenberg 3 of 6/Alamy; p. 68 Cultura/Oxford
University Press; p. 72 Ashley Cooper/Corbis UK Ltd.; p. 72/73 Scott
Rothstein/Shutterstock; p. 73 Tetra Images/Alamy (masks); p. 73 Bettmann/
Corbis UK Ltd. (brothers); p. 73 mozcann/iStockphoto (ipad); p. 74 Silke
Woweries/Corbis UK Ltd. (mother son); p. 74 Sollina Images/Getty Images
(boys); p. 74 wavebreakmedia/Shutterstock (girl); p. 74 Kidstock/Blend
Images/Corbis UK Ltd. (mother daughter); p. 77 Roman Sorkin/Shutterstock;
p. 82 zhang bo/Getty Images; p. 87 Larry Williams and Associates//Corbis
UK Ltd.; p. 89 BLOOMimage/Oxford University Press; p. 92 OJO Images Ltd/
Alamy; p. 96 jocic/Shutterstock (football); p. 96 Chris Crisman/Corbis UK Ltd.
(racing crew); p. 97 Terry J Alcorn/iStockphoto (coach); p. 97 Africa Studio/
Shutterstock (tennis); p. 98 STOCK4B GmbH/Alamy (football); p. 98 Gari Wyn
Williams/Alamy (swimming); p. 98 Photodisc/Oxford University Press (golf);
p. 98 Herbert Kratky/Shutterstock (hockey); p. 100 Mauricio Lima/AFP/Getty
Images; p. 101 Tom Shaw /Allsport/Getty Images (team photo); p. 101 Paulo
Whitaker/Reuters/Corbis UK Ltd. (football game); p. 105 2013 Renato
Silvestre/Getty Images; p. 107 Caro/Alamy; p. 108 Bob Thomas/Popperfoto/
Getty Images; p. 110 Polka Dot Images/Oxford University Press; p. 116 Image
Source/Oxford University Press; p. 120/121 Eric Audras/Getty Images;
p. 121 Evgeny Karandaev/Shutterstock; p. 124 Ned Frisk Photography/
Corbis UK Ltd.; p. 125 Blend Images/Alamy; p. 126 Image Source/Getty
Images; p. 127 Cultura Creative (RF)/Alamy; p. 139 baranq/Shutterstock;
p. 141 Beyond/Corbis UK Ltd.; p. 146/147 Michael Hevesy/Getty Images;
p. 148 Mark Hamilton/Corbis UK Ltd. (skating); p. 148 moodboard/Getty
Images (shop assistant); p. 148 Jose Luis Pelaez Inc/Getty Images (athlete);
p. 150 Papilio/Alamy; p. 156 Wendle Wright/Alamy; p. 160 YAY Media AS/
Alamy; p. 162 Eternity in an Instant/Getty Images; p. 164 Photodisc/Oxford
University Press; p. 170 Panya ST/Shutterstock (centipede); p. 170 Spaces
Images/Alamy (bridge); p. 171 Weatherstock/Corbis UK Ltd. (lightning);
p. 171 GOLFX/Shutterstock (rollercoaster); p. 172 Martin Harvey/Alamy
(snake); p. 172 iStockphoto/Thinkstock (plane); p. 172 JEFF SMITH/Alamy
(lightning); p. 172 Gwoeii/Shutterstock (edge); p. 181 Rob Bartee/Alamy;
p. 186 Design Pics Inc./Alamy; Back Cover: mozcann/iStockphoto.

SHAPING learning TOGETHER

We would like to acknowledge the teachers from all over the world who participated in the development process and review of the Q series.

Special thanks to our *Q: Skills for Success* Second Edition Topic Advisory Board

Shaker Ali Al-Mohammad, Buraimi University College, Oman; **Dr. Asmaa A. Ebrahim**, University of Sharjah, U.A.E.; **Rachel Batchilder**, College of the North Atlantic, Qatar; **Anil Bayir**, Izmir University, Turkey; **Flora Mcvay Bozkurt**, Maltepe University, Turkey; **Paul Bradley**, University of the Thai Chamber of Commerce Bangkok, Thailand; **Joan Birrell-Bertrand**, University of Manitoba, MB, Canada; **Karen E. Caldwell**, Zayed University, U.A.E.; **Nicole Hammond Carrasquel**, University of Central Florida, FL, U.S.; **Kevin Countryman**, Seneca College of Applied Arts & Technology, ON, Canada; **Julie Crocker**, Arcadia University, NS, Canada; **Marc L. Cummings**, Jefferson Community and Technical College, KY, U.S.; **Rachel DeSanto**, Hillsborough Community College Dale Mabry Campus, FL, U.S.; **Nilüfer Ertürkmen**, Ege University, Turkey; **Sue Fine**, Ras Al Khaimah Women's College (HCT), U.A.E.; **Amina Al Hashami**, Nizwa College of Applied Sciences, Oman; **Stephan Johnson**, Nagoya Shoka Daigaku, Japan; **Sean Kim**, Avalon, South Korea; **Gregory King**, Chubu Daigaku, Japan; **Seran Küçük**, Maltepe University, Turkey; **Jonee De Leon**, VUS, Vietnam; **Carol Lowther**, Palomar College, CA, U.S.; **Erin Harris-MacLeod**, St. Mary's University, NS, Canada; **Angela Nagy**, Maltepe University, Turkey; **Huynh Thi Ai Nguyen**, Vietnam; **Daniel L. Paller**, Kinjo Gakuin University, Japan; **Jangyo Parsons**, Kookmin University, South Korea; **Laila Al Qadhi**, Kuwait University, Kuwait; **Josh Rosenberger**, English Language Institute University of Montana, MT, U.S.; **Nancy Schoenfeld**, Kuwait University, Kuwait; **Jenay Seymour**, Hongik University, South Korea; **Moon-young Son**, South Korea; **Matthew Taylor**, Kinjo Gakuin Daigaku, Japan; **Burcu Tezcan-Unal**, Zayed University, U.A.E.; **Troy Tucker**, Edison State College-Lee Campus, FL, U.S.; **Kris Vicca**, Feng Chia University, Taichung; **Jisook Woo**, Incheon University, South Korea; **Dunya Yenidunya**, Ege University, Turkey

UNITED STATES Marcarena Aguilar, North Harris College, TX; **Rebecca Andrade**, California State University North Ridge, CA; **Lesley Andrews**, Boston University, MA; **Deborah Anholt**, Lewis and Clark College, OR; **Robert Anzelde**, Oakton Community College, IL; **Arlys Arnold**, University of Minnesota, MN; **Marcia Arthur**, Renton Technical College, WA; **Renee Ashmeade**, Passaic County Community College, NJ; **Anne Bachmann**, Clackamas Community College, OR; **Lida Baker**, UCLA, CA; **Ron Balsamo**, Santa Rosa Junior College, CA; **Lori Barkley**, Portland State University, OR; **Eileen Barlow**, SUNY Albany, NY; **Sue Bartch**, Cuyahoga Community College, OH; **Lora Bates**, Oakton High School, VA; **Barbara Batra**, Nassau County Community College, NY; **Nancy Baum**, University of Texas at Arlington, TX; **Rebecca Beck**, Irvine Valley College, CA; **Linda Berendsen**, Oakton Community College, IL; **Jennifer Binckes Lee**, Howard Community College, MD; **Grace Bishop**, Houston Community College, TX; **Jean W. Bodman**, Union County College, NJ; **Virginia Bouchard**, George Mason University, VA; **Kimberley Briesch Sumner**, University of Southern California, CA; **Kevin Brown**, University of California, Irvine, CA; **Laura Brown**, Glendale Community College, CA; **Britta Burton**, Mission College, CA; **Allison L. Callahan**, Harold Washington College, IL; **Gabriela Cambiasso**, Harold Washington College, IL; **Jackie Campbell**, Capistrano Unified School District, CA; **Adele C. Camus**, George Mason University, VA; **Laura Chason**, Savannah College, GA; **Kerry Linder Catana**, Language Studies International, NY; **An Cheng**, Oklahoma State University, OK; **Carole Collins**, North Hampton Community College, PA; **Betty R. Compton**, Intercultural Communications College, HI; **Pamela Couch**, Boston University, MA; **Fernanda Crowe**, Intrax International Institute, CA; **Vicki Curtis**, Santa Cruz, CA; **Margo Czinski**, Washtenaw Community College, MI; **David Dahnke**, Lone Star College, TX; **Gillian M. Dale**, CA; **L. Dalgish**, Concordia College, MN; **Christopher Davis**, John Jay College, NY; **Sherry Davis**, Irvine University, CA; **Natalia de Cuba**, Nassau County Community College, NY; **Sonia Delgadillo**, Sierra College, CA; **Esmeralda Diriye**, Cypress College & Cal Poly, CA; **Marta O. Dmytrenko-Ahrabian**, Wayne State University, MI; **Javier Dominguez**, Central High School, SC; **Jo Ellen Downey-Greer**, Lansing Community College, MI; **Jennifer Duclos**, Boston University, MA; **Yvonne Duncan**, City College of San Francisco, CA; **Paul Dydman**, USC Language Academy, CA; **Anna Eddy**, University of Michigan-Flint, MI; **Zohan El-Gamal**, Glendale Community College, CA; **Jennie Farnell**, University of Connecticut, CT; **Susan Fedors**, Howard Community College, MD; **Valerie Fiechter**, Mission College, CA; **Ashley Fifer**, Nassau County Community College, NY; **Matthew Florence**, Intrax International Institute, CA; **Kathleen Flynn**, Glendale College, CA; **Elizabeth Fonsea**, Nassau County Community College, NY; **Eve Fonseca**, St. Louis Community College, MO; **Elizabeth Foss**, Washtenaw Community College, MI; **Duff C. Galda**, Pima Community College, AZ; **Christiane Galvani**, Houston Community College, TX; **Gretchen Gerber**, Howard Community College, MD; **Ray Gonzalez**, Montgomery College, MD; **Janet Goodwin**, University of California, Los Angeles, CA; **Alyona Gorokhova**, Grossmont College, CA; **John Graney**, Santa Fe College, FL; **Kathleen Green**, Central High School, AZ; **Nancy Hamadou**, Pima Community College-West Campus, AZ; **Webb Hamilton**, De Anza College, San Jose City College, CA; **Janet Harclerode**, Santa Monica Community College, CA; **Sandra Hartmann**, Language and Culture Center, TX; **Kathy Haven**, Mission College, CA; **Roberta Hendrick**, Cuyahoga Community College, OH; **Ginny Heringer**, Pasadena City College, CA; **Adam Henricksen**, University of Maryland, MD; **Carolyn Ho**, Lone Star College-CyFair, TX; **Peter Hoffman**, LaGuardia Community College, NY; **Linda Holden**, College of Lake County, IL; **Jana Holt**, Lake Washington Technical College, WA; **Antonio Iccarino**, Boston University, MA; **Gail Ibele**, University of Wisconsin, WI; **Nina Ito**, American Language Institute, CSU Long Beach, CA; **Linda Jensen**, UCLA, CA; **Lisa Jurkowitz**, Pima Community College, CA; **Mandy Kama**, Georgetown University, Washington, DC; **Stephanie Kasuboski**, Cuyahoga Community College, OH; **Chigusa Katoku**, Mission College, CA; **Sandra Kawamura**, Sacramento City College, CA; **Gail Kellersberger**, University of Houston-Downtown, TX; **Jane Kelly**, Durham Technical Community College, NC; **Maryanne Kildare**, Nassau County Community College, NY; **Julie Park Kim**, George Mason University, VA; **Kindra Kinyon**, Los Angeles Trade-Technical College, CA; **Matt Kline**, El Camino College, CA; **Lisa Kovacs-Morgan**, University of California, San Diego, CA; **Claudia Kupiec**, DePaul University, IL; **Renee La Rue**, Lone Star College-Montgomery, TX; **Janet Langon**, Glendale College, CA; **Lawrence Lawson**, Palomar College, CA; **Rachele Lawton**, The Community College of Baltimore County, MD; **Alice Lee**, Richland College, TX; **Esther S. Lee**, CSUF & Mt. SAC, CA; **Cherie Lenz-Hackett**, University of Washington, WA; **Joy Leventhal**, Cuyahoga Community College, OH; **Alice Lin**, UCI Extension, CA; **Monica Lopez**, Cerritos College, CA; **Dustin Lovell**, FLS International Marymount College, CA; **Carol Lowther**, Palomar College, CA; **Candace Lynch-Thompson**, North Orange County Community College District, CA; **Thi Thi Ma**, City College of San Francisco, CA; **Steve Mac Isaac**, USC Long Academy, CA; **Denise Maduli-Williams**, City College of San Francisco, CA; **Eileen Mahoney**, Camelback High School, AZ; **Naomi Mardock**, MCC-Omaha, NE; **Brigitte Maronde**, Harold Washington College, IL; **Marilyn Marquis**, Laposita College CA; **Doris Martin**, Glendale Community College; Pasadena City College, CA; **Keith Maurice**, University of Texas at Arlington, TX; **Nancy Mayer**, University of Missouri-St. Louis, MO; **Aziah McNamara**, Kansas State University, KS; **Billie McQuillan**, Education Heights, MN; **Karen Merritt**, Glendale Union High School District, AZ; **Holly Milkowart**, Johnson County Community College, KS; **Eric Moyer**, Intrax International Institute, CA; **Gino Muzzatti**, Santa Rosa Junior College, CA; **Sandra Navarro**, Glendale Community College, CA; **Than Nyeinkhin**, ELAC, PCC, CA; **William Nedrow**, Triton College, IL; **Eric Nelson**, University of Minnesota, MN; **Than Nyeinkhin**, ELAC, PCC, CA; **Fernanda Ortiz**, Center for English as a Second Language at the University of Arizona, AZ; **Rhony Ory**, Ygnacio Valley High School, CA; **Paul Parent**, Montgomery College, MD; **Dr. Sumeeta Patnaik**, Marshall University, WV; **Oscar Pedroso**, Miami Dade College, FL; **Robin Persiani**, Sierra College, CA; **Patricia Prenz-Belkin**, Hostos Community College, NY; **Suzanne Powell**, University of Louisville, KY; **Jim Ranalli**, Iowa State University, IA; **Toni R. Randall**, Santa Monica College, CA; **Vidya Rangachari**, Mission College, CA; **Elizabeth Rasmussen**, Northern Virginia Community College, VA; **Lara Ravitch**, Truman College, IL;

Deborah Repasz, San Jacinto College, TX; **Marisa Recinos**, English Language Center, Brigham Young University, UT; **Andrey Reznikov**, Black Hills State University, SD; **Alison Rice**, Hunter College, NY; **Jennifer Robles**, Ventura Unified School District, CA; **Priscilla Rocha**, Clark County School District, NV; **Dzidra Rodins**, DePaul University, IL; **Maria Rodriguez**, Central High School, AZ; **Josh Rosenberger**, English Language Institute University of Montana, MT; **Alice Rosso**, Bucks County Community College, PA; **Rita Rozzi**, Xavier University, OH; **Maria Ruiz**, Victor Valley College, CA; **Kimberly Russell**, Clark College, WA; **Stacy Sabraw**, Michigan State University, MI; **Irene Sakk**, Northwestern University, IL; **Deborah Sandstrom**, University of Illinois at Chicago, IL; **Jenni Santamaria**, ABC Adult, CA; **Shaeley Santiago**, Ames High School, IA; **Peg Sarosy**, San Francisco State University, CA; **Alice Savage**, North Harris College, TX; **Donna Schaeffer**, University of Washington, WA; **Karen Marsh Schaeffer**, University of Utah, UT; **Carol Schinger**, Northern Virginia Community College, VA; **Robert Scott**, Kansas State University, KS; **Suell Scott**, Sheridan Technical Center, FL; **Shira Seaman**, Global English Academy, NY; **Richard Seltzer**, Glendale Community College, CA; **Harlan Sexton**, CUNY Queensborough Community College, NY; **Kathy Sherak**, San Francisco State University, CA; **German Silva**, Miami Dade College, FL; **Ray Smith**, Maryland English Institute, University of Maryland, MD; **Shira Smith**, NICE Program University of Hawaii, HI; **Tara Smith**, Felician College, NJ; **Monica Snow**, California State University, Fullerton, CA; **Elaine Soffer**, Nassau County Community College, NY; **Andrea Spector**, Santa Monica Community College, CA; **Jacqueline Sport**, LBWCC Luverne Center, AL; **Karen Stanely**, Central Piedmont Community College, NC; **Susan Stern**, Irvine Valley College, CA; **Ayse Stromsdorfer**, Soldan I.S.H.S., MO; **Yilin Sun**, South Seattle Community College, WA; **Thomas Swietlik**, Intrax International Institute, IL; **Nicholas Taggert**, University of Dayton, OH; **Judith Tanka**, UCLA Extension–American Language Center, CA; **Amy Taylor**, The University of Alabama Tuscaloosa, AL; **Andrea Taylor**, San Francisco State, CA; **Priscilla Taylor**, University of Southern California, CA; **Ilene Teixeira**, Fairfax County Public Schools, VA; **Shirl H. Terrell**, Collin College, TX; **Marya Teutsch-Dwyer**, St. Cloud State University, MN; **Stephen Thergesen**, ELS Language Centers, CO; **Christine Tierney**, Houston Community College, TX; **Arlene Turini**, North Moore High School, NC; **Cara Tuzzolino**, Nassau County Community College, NY; **Suzanne Van Der Valk**, Iowa State University, IA; **Nathan D. Vasarhely**, Ygnacio Valley High School, CA; **Naomi S. Verratti**, Howard Community College, MD; **Hollyahna Vettori**, Santa Rosa Junior College, CA; **Julie Vorholt**, Lewis & Clark College, OR; **Danielle Wagner**, FLS International Marymount College, CA; **Lynn Walker**, Coastline College, CA; **Laura Walsh**, City College of San Francisco, CA; **Andrew J. Watson**, The English Bakery; **Donald Weasenforth**, Collin College, TX; **Juliane Widner**, Sheepshead Bay High School, NY; **Lynne Wilkins**, Mills College, CA; **Pamela Williams**, Ventura College, CA; **Jeff Wilson**, Irvine Valley College, CA; **James Wilson**, Consomnes River College, CA; **Katie Windahl**, Cuyahoga Community College, OH; **Dolores "Lorrie" Winter**, California State University at Fullerton, CA; **Jody Yamamoto**, Kapi'olani Community College, HI; **Ellen L. Yaniv**, Boston University, MA; **Norman Yoshida**, Lewis & Clark College, OR; **Joanna Zadra**, American River College, CA; **Florence Zysman**, Santiago Canyon College, CA;

CANADA Patricia Birch, Brandon University, MB; **Jolanta Caputa**, College of New Caledonia, BC; **Katherine Coburn**, UBC's ELI, BC; **Erin Harris-Macleod**, St. Mary's University, NS; **Tami Moffatt**, English Language Institute, BC; **Jim Papple**, Brock University, ON; **Robin Peace**, Confederation College, BC;

ASIA Rabiatu Abubakar, Eton Language Centre, Malaysia; **Wiwik Andreani**, Bina Nusantara University, Indonesia; **Frank Bailey**, Baiko Gakuin University, Japan; **Mike Baker**, Kosei Junior High School, Japan; **Leonard Barrow**, Kanto Junior College, Japan; **Herman Bartelen**, Japan; **Siren Betty**, Fooyin University, Kaohsiung; **Thomas E. Bieri**, Nagoya College, Japan; **Natalie Brezden**, Global English House, Japan; **MK Brooks**, Mukogawa Women's University, Japan; **Truong Ngoc Buu**, The Youth Language School, Vietnam; **Charles Cabell**, Toyo University, Japan; **Fred Carruth**, Matsumoto University, Japan; **Frances Causer**, Seijo University, Japan; **Jeffrey Chalk**, SNU, South Korea; **Deborah Chang**, Wenzao Ursuline College of Languages, Kaohsiung; **David Chatham**, Ritsumeikan University, Japan; **Andrew Chih Hong Chen**, National Sun Yat-sen University, Kaohsiung; **Christina Chen**, Yu-Tsai Bilingual Elementary School, Taipei; **Hui-chen Chen**, Shi-Lin High School of Commerce, Taipei; **Seungmoon Choe**, K2M Language Institute, South Korea; **Jason Jeffree Cole**, Coto College, Japan; **Le Minh Cong**, Vungtau Tourism Vocational College, Vietnam; **Todd Cooper**, Toyama National College of Technology, Japan; **Marie Cosgrove**, Daito Bunka

University, Japan; **Randall Cotten**, Gifu City Women's College, Japan; **Tony Cripps**, Ritsumeikan University, Japan; **Andy Cubalit**, CHS, Thailand; **Daniel Cussen**, Takushoku University, Japan; **Le Dan**, Ho Chi Minh City Electric Power College, Vietnam; **Simon Daykin**, Banghwa-dong Community Centre, South Korea; **Aimee Denham**, ILA, Vietnam; **Bryan Dickson**, David's English Center, Taipei; **Nathan Ducker**, Japan University, Japan; **Ian Duncan**, Simul International Corporate Training, Japan; **Nguyen Thi Kieu Dung**, Thang Long University, Vietnam; **Truong Quang Dung**, Tien Giang University, Vietnam; **Nguyen Thi Thuy Duong**, Vietnamese American Vocational Training College, Vietnam; **Wong Tuck Ee**, Raja Tun Azlan Science Secondary School, Malaysia; **Emilia Effendy**, International Islamic University Malaysia, Malaysia; **Bettizza Escueta**, KMUTT, Thailand; **Robert Eva**, Kaisei Girls High School, Japan; **Jim George**, Luna International Language School, Japan; **Jurgen Germeys**, Silk Road Language Center, South Korea; **Wong Ai Gnoh**, SMJK Chung Hwa Confucian, Malaysia; **Sarah Go**, Seoul Women's University, South Korea; **Peter Goosselink**, Hokkai High School, Japan; **Robert Gorden**, SNU, South Korea; **Wendy M. Gough**, St. Mary College/Nunoike Gaigo Senmon Gakko, Japan; **Tim Grose**, Sapporo Gakuin University, Japan; **Pham Thu Ha**, Le Van Tam Primary School, Vietnam; **Ann-Marie Hadzima**, Taipei; **Troy Hammond**, Tokyo Gakugei University International Secondary School, Japan; **Robiatul 'Adawiah Binti Hamzah**, SMK Putrajaya Precinct 8(1), Malaysia; **Tran Thi Thuy Hang**, Ho Chi Minh City Banking University, Vietnam; **To Thi Hong Hanh**, CEFALT, Vietnam; **George Hays**, Tokyo Kokusai Daigaku, Japan; **Janis Hearn**, Hongik University, South Korea; **Chantel Hemmi**, Jochi Daigaku, Japan; **David Hindman**, Sejong University, South Korea; **Nahn Cam Hoa**, Ho Chi Minh City University of Technology, Vietnam; **Jana Holt**, Korea University, South Korea; **Jason Hollowell**, Nihon University, Japan; **F. N. (Zoe) Hsu**, National Tainan University, Yong Kang; **Kuei-ping Hsu**, National Tsing Hua University, Hsinchu City; **Wenhua Hsu**, I-Shou University, Kaohsiung; **Luu Nguyen Quoc Hung**, Cantho University, Vietnam; **Cecile Hwang**, Changwon National University, South Korea; **Ainol Haryati Ibrahim**, Universiti Malaysia Pahang, Malaysia; **Robert Jeens**, Yonsei University, South Korea; **Linda M. Joyce**, Kyushu Sangyo University, Japan; **Dr. Nisai Kaewsanchai**, English Square Kanchanaburi, Thailand; **Aniza Kamarulzaman**, Sabah Science Secondary School, Malaysia; **Ikuko Kashiwabara**, Osaka Electro-Communication University, Japan; **Gurmit Kaur**, INTI College, Malaysia; **Nick Keane**, Japan; **Ward Ketcheson**, Aomori University, Japan; **Nicholas Kemp**, Kyushu International University, Japan; **Montchatry Ketmuni**, Rajamangala University of Technology, Thailand; **Dinh Viet Khanh**, Japan; **Seonok Kim**, Kangsu Jongro Language School, South Korea; **Suyeon Kim**, Anyang University, South Korea; **Kelly P. Kimura**, Soka University, Japan; **Masakazu Kimura**, Katoh Gakuen Gyoshu High School, Japan; **Gregory King**, Chubu Daigaku, Japan; **Stan Kirk**, Konan University, Japan; **Donald Knight**, Nan Hua/Fu Li Junior High Schools, Hsinchu; **Kari J. Kostiainen**, Nagoya City University, Japan; **Pattri Kuanpulpol**, Silpakorn University, Thailand; **Ha Thi Lan**, Thai Binh Teacher Training College, Vietnam; **Eric Edwin Larson**, Miyazaki Prefectural Nursing University, Japan; **David Laurence**, Chubu Daigaku, Japan; **Richard S. Lavin**, Prefectural University of Kumamoto, Japan; **Shirley Leane**, Chugoku Junior College, Japan; **I-Hsiu Lee**, Yunlin; **Nari Lee**, Park Jung PLS, South Korea; **Tae Lee**, Yonsei University, South Korea; **Lys Yongsoon Lee**, Reading Town Geumcheon, South Korea; **Mallory Leece**, Sun Moon University, South Korea; **Dang Hong Lien**, Tan Lam Upper Secondary School, Vietnam; **Huang Li-Han**, Rebecca Education Institute, Taipei; **Sovannarith Lim**, Royal University of Phnom Penh, Cambodia; **Ginger Lin**, National Kaohsiung Hospitality College, Kaohsiung; **Noel Lineker**, New Zealand/Japan; **Tran Dang Khanh Linh**, Nha Trang Teachers' Training College, Vietnam; **Daphne Liu**, Buliton English School, Taipei; **S. F. Josephine Liu**, Tien-Mu Elementary School, Taipei ; **Caroline Luo**, Tunghai University, Taichung; **Jeng-Jia Luo**, Tunghai University, Taichung; **Laura MacGregor**, Gakushuin University, Japan; **Amir Madani**, Visuttharangsi School, Thailand; **Elena Maeda**, Sacred Heart Professional Training College, Japan; **Vu Thi Thanh Mai**, Hoang Gia Education Center, Vietnam; **Kimura Masakazu**, Kato Gakuen Gyoshu High School, Japan; **Susumu Matsuhashi**, Net Link English School, Japan; **James McCrostie**, Daito Bunka University, Japan; **Joel McKee**, Inha University, South Korea; **Colin McKenzie**, Wachirawit Primary School, Thailand; **Terumi Miyazoe**, Tokyo Denki Daigaku, Japan; **William K. Moore**, Hiroshima Kokusai Gakuin University, Japan; **Kevin Mueller**, Tokyo Kokusai Daigaku, Japan; **Hudson Murrell**, Baiko Gakuin University, Japan; **Frances Namba**, Senri International School of Kwansei Gakuin, Japan; **Keiichi Narita**, Niigata University, Japan; **Kim Chung Nguyen**, Ho Chi Minh University of

iv

Industry, Vietnam; **Do Thi Thanh Nhan**, Hanoi University, Vietnam; **Dale Kazuo Nishi**, Aoyama English Conversation School, Japan; **Huynh Thi Ai Nguyen**, Vietnam; **Dongshin Oh**, YBM PLS, South Korea; **Keiko Okada**, Dokkyo Daigaku, Japan; **Louise Ohashi**, Shukutoku University, Japan; **Yongjun Park**, Sangji University, South Korea; **Donald Patnaude**, Ajarn Donald's English Language Services, Thailand; **Virginia Peng**, Ritsumeikan University, Japan; **Suangkanok Piboonthamnont**, Rajamangala University of Technology, Thailand; **Simon Pitcher**, Business English Teaching Services, Japan; **John C. Probert**, New Education Worldwide, Thailand; **Do Thi Hoa Quyen**, Ton Duc Thang University, Vietnam; **John P. Racine**, Dokkyo University, Japan; **Kevin Ramsden**, Kyoto University of Foreign Studies, Japan; **Luis Rappaport**, Cung Thieu Nha Ha Noi, Vietnam; **Lisa Reshad**, Konan Daigaku Hyogo, Japan; **Peter Riley**, Taisho University, Japan; **Thomas N. Robb**, Kyoto Sangyo University, Japan; **Rory Rosszell**, Meiji Daigaku, Japan; **Maria Feti Rosyani**, Universitas Kristen Indonesia, Indonesia; **Greg Rouault**, Konan University, Japan; **Chris Ruddenklau**, Kindai University, Japan; **Hans-Gustav Schwartz**, Thailand; **Mary-Jane Scott**, Soongsil University, South Korea; **Dara Sheahan**, Seoul National University, South Korea; **James Sherlock**, A.P.W. Angthong, Thailand; **Prof. Shieh**, Minghsin University of Science & Technology, Xinfeng; **Yuko Shimizu**, Ritsumeikan University, Japan; **Suzila Mohd Shukor**, Universiti Sains Malaysia, Malaysia; **Stephen E. Smith**, Mahidol University, Thailand; **Moon-young Son**, South Korea; **Seunghee Son**, Anyang University, South Korea; **Mi-young Song**, Kyungwon University, South Korea; **Lisa Sood**, VUS, BIS, Vietnam; **Jason Stewart**, Taejon International Language School, South Korea; **Brian A. Stokes**, Korea University, South Korea; **Mulder Su**, Shih-Chien University, Kaohsiung; **Yoomi Suh**, English Plus, South Korea; **Yun-Fang Sun**, Wenzao Ursuline College of Languages, Kaohsiung; **Richard Swingle**, Kansai Gaidai University, Japan; **Sanford Taborn**, Kinjo Gakuin Daigaku, Japan; **Mamoru Takahashi**, Akita Prefectural University, Japan; **Tran Hoang Tan**, School of International Training, Vietnam; **Takako Tanaka**, Doshisha University, Japan; **Jeffrey Taschner**, American University Alumni Language Center, Thailand; **Matthew Taylor**, Kinjo Gakuin Daigaku, Japan; **Michael Taylor**, International Pioneers School, Thailand; **Kampanart Thammaphati**, Wattana Wittaya Academy, Thailand; **Tran Duong The**, Sao Mai Language Center, Vietnam; **Tran Dinh Tho**, Duc Tri Secondary School, Vietnam; **Huynh Thi Anh Thu**, Nhatrang College of Culture Arts and Tourism, Vietnam; **Peter Timmins**, Peter's English School, Japan; **Fumie Togano**, Hosei Daini High School, Japan; **F. Sigmund Topor**, Keio University Language School, Japan; **Tu Trieu**, Rise VN, Vietnam; **Yen-Cheng Tseng**, Chang-Jung Christian University, Tainan; **Pei-Hsuan Tu**, National Cheng Kung University, Tainan City; **Hajime Uematsu**, Hirosaki University, Japan; **Rachel Um**, Mok-dong Oedae English School, South Korea; **David Underhill**, EEExpress, Japan; **Ben Underwood**, Kugenuma High School, Japan; **Siriluck Usaha**, Sripatum University, Thailand; **Tyas Budi Utami**, Indonesia; **Nguyen Thi Van**, Far East International School, Vietnam; **Stephan Van Eycken**, Kosei Gakuen Girls High School, Japan; **Zisa Velasquez**, Taihu International School/Semarang International School, China/Indonesia; **Jeffery Walter**, Sangji University, South Korea; **Bill White**, Kinki University, Japan; **Yohanes De Deo Widyastoko**, Xaverius Senior High School, Indonesia; **Dylan Williams**, SNU, South Korea; **Jisuk Woo**, Ichean University, South Korea; **Greg Chung-Hsien Wu**, Providence University, Taichung; **Xun Xiaoming**, BLCU, China; **Hui-Lien Yeh**, Chai Nan University of Pharmacy and Science, Tainan; **Sittiporn Yodnil**, Huachiew Chalermprakiet University, Thailand; **Shamshul Helmy Zambahari**, Universiti Teknologi Malaysia, Malaysia; **Ming-Yuli**, Chang Jung Christian University, Tainan; **Aimin Fadhlee bin Mahmud Zuhodi**, Kuala Terengganu Science School, Malaysia;

TURKEY **Shirley F. Akis**, American Culture Association/Fomara; **Gül Akkoç**, Boğaziçi University; **Seval Akmeşe**, Haliç University; **Ayşenur Akyol**, Ege University; **Ayşe Umut Aribaş**, Beykent University; **Gökhan Asan**, Kapadokya Vocational College; **Hakan Asan**, Kapadokya Vocational College; **Julia Asan**, Kapadokya Vocational College; **Azarvan Atac**, Piri Reis University; **Nur Babat**, Kapadokya Vocational College; **Feyza Balakbabalar**, Kadir Has University; **Gözde Balikçi**, Beykent University; **Deniz Balım**, Haliç University; **Asli Başdoğan**, Kadir Has University; **Ayla Bayram**, Kapadokya Vocational College; **Pinar Bilgiç**, Kadir Has University; **Kenan Bozkurt**, Kapadokya Vocational College; **Yonca Bozkurt**, Ege University; **Frank Carr**, Piri Reis; **Mengü Noyan Çengel**, Ege University; **Elif Doğan**, Ege University; **Natalia Donmez**, 29 Mayis Üniverste; **Nalan Emirsoy**, Kadir Has University; **Ayşe Engin**, Kadir Has University; **Ayhan Gedikbaş**, Ege University; **Gülşah Gençer**, Beykent University; **Seyit Ömer Gök**, Gediz University; **Tuğba Gök**, Gediz University; **İlkay Gökçe**, Ege University; **Zeynep Birinci Guler**, Maltepe University; **Neslihan Güler**, Kadir Has University; **Sircan Gümüş**, Kadir Has University; **Nesrin Gündoğu**, T.C. Piri Reis University; **Tanju Gurpinar**, Piri Reis University; **Selin Gurturk**, Piri Reis University; **Neslihan Gurutku**, Piri Reis University; **Roger Hewitt**, Maltepe University; **Nilüfer İbrahimoğlu**, Beykent University; **Nevin Kaftelen**, Kadir Has University; **Sultan Kalin**, Kapadokya Vocational College; **Sema Kaplan Karabina**, Anadolu University; **Eray Kara**, Giresun University; **Beylü Karayazgan**, Ege University; **Darren Kelso**, Piri Reis University; **Trudy Kittle**, Kapadokya Vocational College; **Şaziye Konaç**, Kadir Has University; **Güneş Korkmaz**, Kapadokya Vocational College; **Robert Ledbury**, Izmir University of Economics; **Ashley Lucas**, Maltepe University; **Bülent Nedium Uça**, Dogus University; **Murat Nurlu**, Ege University; **Mollie Owens**, Kadir Has University; **Oya Özağaç**, Boğaziçi University; **Funda Özcan**, Ege University; **İlkay Özdemir**, Ege University; **Ülkü Öztürk**, Gediz University; **Cassondra Puls**, Anadolu University; **Yelda Sarikaya**, Cappadocia Vocational College; **Müge Şekercioğlu**, Ege University; **Melis Senol**, Canakkale Onsekiz Mart University, The School of Foreign Languages; **Patricia Sümer**, Kadir Has University; **Rex Surface**, Beykent University; **Mustafa Torun**, Kapadokya Vocational College; **Tansel Üstünloğlu**, Ege University; **Fatih Yücel**, Beykent University; **Şule Yüksel**, Piri Reis University;

THE MIDDLE EAST **Amina Saif Mohammed Al Hashamia**, Nizwa College of Applied Sciences, Oman; **Jennifer Baran**, Kuwait University, Kuwait; **Phillip Chappells**, GEMS Modern Academy, U.A.E.; **Sharon Ruth Devaneson**, Ibri College of Technology, Oman; **Hanaa El-Deeb**, Canadian International College, Egypt; **Yvonne Eaton**, Community College of Qatar, Qatar; **Brian Gay**, Sultan Qaboos University, Oman; **Gail Al Hafidh**, Sharjah Women's College (HCT), U.A.E.; **Jonathan Hastings**, American Language Center, Jordan; **Laurie Susan Hilu**, English Language Centre, University of Bahrain, Bahrain; **Abraham Irannezhad**, Mehre Aval, Iran; **Kevin Kempe**, CNA-Q, Qatar; **Jill Newby James**, University of Nizwa; **Mary Kay Klein**, American University of Sharjah, U.A.E.; **Sian Khoury**, Fujairah Women's College (HCT), U.A.E.; **Hussein Dehghan Manshadi**, Farhang Pajooh & Jaam-e-Jam Language School, Iran; **Jessica March**, American University of Sharjah, U.A.E.; **Neil McBeath**, Sultan Qaboos University, Oman; **Sandy McDonagh**, Abu Dhabi Men's College (HCT), U.A.E.; **Rob Miles**, Sharjah Women's College (HCT), U.A.E.; **Michael Kevin Neumann**, Al Ain Men's College (HCT), U.A.E.;

LATIN AMERICA **Aldana Aguirre**, Argentina; **Claudia Almeida**, Coordenação de Idiomas, Brazil; **Cláudia Arias**, Brazil; **Maria de los Angeles Barba**, FES Acatlan UNAM, Mexico; **Lilia Barrios**, Universidad Autónoma de Tamaulipas, Mexico; **Adán Beristain**, UAEM, Mexico; **Ricardo Böck**, Manoel Ribas, Brazil; **Edson Braga**, CNA, Brazil; **Marli Buttelli**, Mater et Magistra, Brazil; **Alessandra Campos**, Inova Centro de Linguas, Brazil; **Priscila Catta Preta Ribeiro**, Brazil; **Gustavo Cestari**, Access International School, Brazil; **Walter D'Alessandro**, Virginia Language Center, Brazil; **Lilian De Gennaro**, Argentina; **Mônica De Stefani**, Quality Centro de Idiomas, Brazil; **Julio Alejandro Flores**, BUAP, Mexico; **Mirian Freire**, CNA Vila Guilherme, Brazil; **Francisco Garcia**, Colegio Lestonnac de San Angel, Mexico; **Miriam Giovanardi**, Brazil; **Darlene Gonzalez Miy**, ITESM CCV, Mexico; **Maria Laura Grimaldi**, Argentina; **Luz Dary Guzmán**, IMPAHU, Colombia; **Carmen Koppe**, Brazil; **Monica Krutzler**, Brazil; **Marcus Murilo Lacerda**, Seven Idiomas, Brazil; **Nancy Lake**, CEL-LEP, Brazil; **Cris Lazzerini**, Brazil; **Sandra Luna**, Argentina; **Ricardo Luvisan**, Brazil; **Jorge Murilo Menezes**, ACBEU, Brazil; **Monica Navarro**, Instituto Cultural A. C., Mexico; **Joacyr Oliveira**, Faculdades Metropolitanas Unidas and Summit School for Teachers, Brazil; **Ayrton Cesar Oliveira de Araujo**, E&A English Classes, Brazil; **Ana Laura Oriente**, Seven Idiomas, Brazil; **Adelia Peña Clavel**, CELE UNAM, Mexico; **Beatriz Pereira**, Summit School, Brazil; **Miguel Perez**, Instituto Cultural, Mexico; **Cristiane Perone**, Associação Cultura Inglesa, Brazil; **Pamela Claudia Pogré**, Colegio Integral Caballito / Universidad de Flores, Argentina; **Dalva Prates**, Brazil; **Marianne Rampaso**, Iowa Idiomas, Brazil; **Daniela Rutolo**, Instituto Superior Cultural Británico, Argentina; **Maione Sampaio**, Maione Carrijo Consultoria em Inglês Ltda, Brazil; **Elaine Santesso**, TS Escola de Idiomas, Brazil; **Camila Francisco Santos**, UNS Idiomas, Brazil; **Lucia Silva**, Cooplem Idiomas, Brazil; **Maria Adela Sorzio**, Instituto Superior Santa Cecilia, Argentina; **Elcio Souza**, Unibero, Brazil; **Willie Thomas**, Rainbow Idiomas, Brazil; **Sandra Villegas**, Instituto Humberto de Paolis, Argentina; **John Whelan**, La Universidad Nacional Autonoma de Mexico, Mexico

CONTENTS

READING ▶ previewing a text
VOCABULARY ▶ word forms
WRITING ▶ writing a main idea and supporting sentences
GRAMMAR ▶ verbs + infinitives (*like*, *want*, and *need*)

UNIT QUESTION

What is a good job?

A Discuss these questions with your classmates.

1. Look at the photo. Where is the woman working? What is she doing? Does this look like a good job to you?

2. Do you have a job now? Do you think it is a good job?

3. Why is it important to have a good job?

B Listen to *The Q Classroom* online. Then answer these questions.

1. What do the students say?

2. Do you agree or disagree with them? Why?

 C Go to the Online Discussion Board to discuss the Unit Question with your classmates.

D Work with a partner. Match each job with a picture.

chef	doctor	sales clerk
construction worker	office worker	truck driver

1. _____

2. _____

3. _____

4. _____

5. _____

6. _____

E Ask your partner the questions about each job above.

1. Does someone you know have this job?

2. Is it a good job? Why or why not?

READING 1 | **The Right Job for You**

UNIT OBJECTIVE You are going to read a Web page for people who are looking for work. Use the Web page to gather information and ideas for your Unit Assignment.

PREVIEW THE READING

Tip for Success

Sometimes you can find the meaning of a new word by understanding the meaning of the other words around it. These are called *context clues*. Look at the grammar and punctuation, too.

A. **VOCABULARY** Here are some words from Reading 1. Read the sentences. Then write each <u>underlined</u> word next to the correct definition.

1. He had a 30-year <u>career</u> as a doctor at City Hospital.

2. We always <u>plan</u> our August vacation in June. We decide where to go.

3. I wish you <u>success</u> in your new job.

4. Good doctors have the <u>skill</u> to help sick people.

5. The job center tries to <u>match</u> people and jobs, so people are happy in their jobs.

6. It is a difficult problem. I cannot <u>solve</u> it.

7. They have new ideas all the time. They are very <u>creative</u>.

8. I have a difficult <u>decision</u>. Do I get a job or go to college?

a. _____ (*verb*) to decide what you are going to do and how

b. _____ (*verb*) to find the answer to a problem

c. _____ (*noun*) a choice that you make after thinking

d. _____ (*noun*) a job that you learn to do and then do for many years

e. _____ (*noun*) getting what you want, doing well

f. _____ (*noun*) something you do well

g. _____ (*verb*) to put together two things that belong together

h. _____ (*adjective*) having a lot of new ideas

iQ ONLINE **B.** Go online for more practice with the vocabulary.

C. **QUICK WRITE** What are your interests? Write five things you like to do. Remember to use this section for your Unit Assignment.

Good readers **preview** a text (for example, an article, a Web page, or a story) before reading it. They look quickly at the text and its different parts. This helps them understand it. Here are some tips to help you preview.

- Read the **title**. The title is the name of the text.
- Read the **headings**. A heading is a short line of text. It tells what a section is about. Often there is a heading above each section.
- Look at any pictures and their **captions**. A caption is the text under the picture.

D. PREVIEW This is a Web page for people who are looking for work. Preview the Web page. Then complete the sentences.

1. This is the Web page of a _____.
   a. university   b. career center   c. newspaper

2. This website is useful if you want _____.
   a. a job   b. a school   c. an office

3. The Web page has _____ steps.
   a. two   b. three   c. four

 E. Go online for more practice with previewing a text.

WORK WITH THE READING

A. Read the Web page. Gather information about what a good job is.

Winter Hill Career Center

The Right Job for You

What kind of work do you want? What are your **skills**? What are your interests?

The Winter Hill **Career** Center can help you choose a career!

After you take the test, meet with us. We can help you find work that **matches** your skills and interests.

Step 1: Take the career test.

This is the Winter Hill Career Center test. It matches you with possible careers. It is important that your skills and interests match your career. Happy workers have more **success**. Check (✓) your skills and interests to find your worker type[1].

Type 1	☐ I like to be **outside**. ☐ I am good with my hands. ☐ I fix things around the house.	Type 4	☐ I like to talk to different people. ☐ I often plan activities. ☐ I like to help people.
Type 2	☐ I like to **solve** problems. ☐ I like to learn new information. ☐ I like science.	Type 5	☐ I like to talk. ☐ People usually listen to me. ☐ I make **decisions** easily.
Type 3	☐ I like poetry. ☐ I often talk about feelings. ☐ I am **creative**.	Type 6	☐ I follow directions carefully. ☐ I am good with details. ☐ I am good with numbers.

Step 2: Choose possible careers.

Which type of worker are you? Look at the boxes with checks (✓). Any section with two or three check marks is your type. Look below for some possible careers for your worker type. Do any of the careers look good to you? We can help you decide.

Type 1: **carpenter, construction worker** Type 2: **doctor, computer programmer** Type 3: **chef, hairdresser** Type 4: **nurse, teacher** Type 5: **lawyer, business person** Type 6: **accountant, office manager**

Step 3: Visit us to plan your career.

---

[1] **worker type:** a group of interests or skills that make a person good for a certain career or job

B. According to the Winter Hill Career Center, there are three steps to finding the right job. Put the steps in the correct order.

___ Go to the Winter Hill Career Center.

___ Check your skills and interests.

___ Look at careers that match your skills and interests.

Tip for Success

To help you answer a question by scanning, underline important words in the question. Scanning for those words makes it easy to find the information.

C. Which career matches each person's skills and interests? Scan the career test and possible careers in Reading 1. Then circle the correct answers.

1. I like to help people. I often plan activities.
   a. teacher
   b. carpenter

2. I like to talk. I make decisions easily.
   a. accountant
   b. lawyer

3. I'm good with numbers. I follow directions carefully.
   a. accountant
   b. teacher

4. I'm creative. I like art, music, and movies.
   a. hairdresser
   b. nurse

5. I like science. I like to learn new information.
   a. computer programmer
   b. construction worker

6. I'm good with my hands. I like to be outside.
   a. chef
   b. carpenter

D. Look at the six occupations. Which worker types do they match? Add them to the chart on page 9.

farmer

science professor

fashion designer

personal trainer

bank teller

salesperson

Type	Interests and Skills	Occupations
1	I like to be outside. I am good with my hands. I like to fix things.	construction worker
2	I like to solve problems. I like to learn new information. I like science.	computer programmer
3	I like art, music, and movies. I often talk about feelings. I like to try new ideas.	chef
4	I like to talk to different people. I often plan activities. I like to help people.	teacher
5	I like to talk. People usually listen to me. I make decisions easily.	business person
6	I follow directions carefully. I am good with details. I am good with numbers.	office manager

E. The reading says, "It is important that your skills and interests match your career." Why is it important? Discuss with a partner.

 WRITE WHAT YOU THINK

A. Take the career test on page 7. Then discuss the questions in Step 2 in a group.

B. What type of worker are you? Write a few sentences explaining your answer. Look back at your Quick Write on page 5. Add anything you learned about yourself from the quiz.

READING 2 | The World of Work

You are going to read interviews in a magazine about different careers. Use the article to gather information and ideas for your Unit Assignment.

PREVIEW THE READING

A. **VOCABULARY** Here are some words from Reading 2. Read their definitions. Then complete each sentence.

> **company** *(noun)* 🔑 a group of people who work together to make or sell things
>
> **customer** *(noun)* 🔑 a person who buys things or services
>
> **event** *(noun)* 🔑 something important or unusual that happens
>
> **flexible** *(adjective)* able to change easily
>
> **product** *(noun)* 🔑 something people make to sell
>
> **regular** *(adjective)* 🔑 happening again and again in the same way
>
> **result** *(noun)* 🔑 something that happens because of something else

🔑 Oxford 2000 keywords

1. Her success is the _____ of many years of hard work.

2. My hours are _____. I always work from 8:00am to 5:00pm, Sunday through Thursday.

3. This job is different every day. That's why we need _____ people.

4. I work for a small _____. There are four people in our office.

5. The new _____ is great. Everyone is buying it!

6. The most important _____ of the year is the company's awards ceremony.

7. The _____ asked the sales assistant many questions.

iQ ONLINE **B.** Go online for more practice with the vocabulary.

Tip for Success

You do not need to understand every word in a reading text. To build your vocabulary, circle the four or five new words you think are most important and find them in the dictionary.

C. **PREVIEW** Preview the interviews. Look at the questions. What information do the people give about their work? Check (✓) your ideas.

☐ 1. the pay

☐ 2. the name of the job

☐ 3. where they work

☐ 4. what they do every day at work

☐ 5. what they do at home

☐ 6. what they like about their work

D. **QUICK WRITE** What do you know about these jobs? What do people with these jobs do? Where do they work? What skills do these jobs require? Remember to use this section for your Unit Assignment.

physical therapist	event planner	sales assistant	Web designer

WORK WITH THE READING

A. Read the interviews. Gather information on what a good job is.

The World of Work

There are many different kinds of work. People enjoy their work for many different reasons. We talked to four people about their work. Read about their careers.

What do you do? I'm a physical therapist. I work in a hospital. **What are your responsibilities?** I help my patients get healthy and stay healthy. I learn about a patient's health problem. I make a plan for the patient. I teach the patient how to exercise and move. **Why do you like your job?** I know my work is important. My patients are nice. I work from 9:00am to 5:00pm, Monday to Friday. I like the **regular** hours.

What do you do? I'm an **event** planner. I work in an office, but I travel a lot.

What are your responsibilities? I plan big events for businesses. I plan the location, the transportation, the food, and the activities for the event. I work with many different people in restaurants, hotels, and transportation. I need to be very organized and remember a lot of details.

Why do you like your job? My work is fun and exciting. I like to meet new people. I like to travel. Also, I see the **results** of my work with every event. That makes me happy.

What do you do? I am a sales assistant in a computer store.

What are your responsibilities? I need to know all about computers. I help **customers** make decisions about what to buy. I explain our **products**.

Why do you like your job? My job is interesting. I like to learn about new products. There is always something new. I work evenings, so I have time at home in the morning with my baby daughter. And the job pays me well.

What do you do? I am a Web designer. I make websites for companies. I am self-employed[1]. I work in my home office.

What are your responsibilities? A **company** asks me to plan a website. I learn about the company and what it needs. I write a plan. I talk to the company again. If they like the plan, I make the website.

Why do you like your job? I like to be creative. I like my quiet home office. Also, I have **flexible** hours. I work when I want. I can say no to a job, too.

[1] **self-employed:** working for yourself, not for somebody else

B. Circle the answer that best completes the statement.

This article helps the reader _____.
a. find a company
b. learn about careers
c. write about their careers

C. Who is speaking? Write the job title from the interviews next to each statement.

1. <u>sales assistant</u> I talk about the different products in our store.

2. _____ I work at home.

3. _____ I help people with health problems.

4. _____ I travel a lot.

5. _____ I help people move and exercise.

6. _____ I need to learn about new products.

7. _____ I have a flexible schedule.

8. _____ I work with patients and doctors in a hospital.

D. Complete the chart with information about each career.

Job Title	Workplace	Work Skills	Work Schedules
Event planner			
Physical therapist			
Sales assistant			
Web designer			

E. Complete the sentences with adjectives from the box.

creative	exciting	important	interesting	quiet

1. The event planner says her work is _____.

2. The physical therapist says his work is _____.

3. The sales assistant says his work is _____.

4. The Web designer says her work is _____ and

    _____.

F. Look back at your Quick Write on page 11. Add new information you learned from the reading.

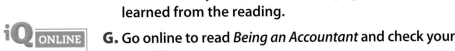 **G.** Go online to read *Being an Accountant* and check your comprehension.

WRITE WHAT YOU THINK

A. Discuss the question in a group. Look back at your Quick Write on page 11 as you think about what you learned.

What is important to you in a job? Check (✓) your answers.

☐ nice people   ☐ regular hours

☐ learning about new products   ☐ being creative

☐ flexible hours   ☐ a quiet workplace

☐ good pay   ☐ solving problems

iQ ONLINE

B. Go online to watch the video about emergency medical technicians. Then check your comprehension.

Writing Tip

Every sentence needs a subject and a verb. The subject is who or what the sentence is about. The verb tells what the subject does or what the subject thinks, feels, or is.

C. Think about the unit video, Reading 1, and Reading 2 as you discuss the questions. Then choose one question and write a response.

1. Which job from Reading 1, Reading 2, or the video do you want to have? Why?

I want to be a(n) _____.

Reason: _____

_____

_____

2. Which job from Reading 1, Reading 2, or the video do you NOT want to have? Why not?

I do not want to be a(n) _____.

Reason: _____

_____

_____

Some words are both **nouns** and **verbs**. They look the same, but they work differently in a sentence. A noun refers to a person, place, object, or idea. A verb refers to an action. Learning to use the same word in different forms helps build your vocabulary.

These words from Reading 1 and Reading 2 can be nouns or verbs.

Word	Noun	Verb
match	This job is a **match** for you.	My skills and interests **match** my career.
plan	His **plan** is to go on vacation next month.	I **plan** activities for people in my office.
result	The **result** of his hard work is a good website.	Hard work **results** in success.
travel	I enjoy **travel**.	I **travel** a lot for my job.
work	There are many different kinds of **work**.	I **work** in a large hospital in the city.

Critical Thinking Tip

In Activity A, you have to **label** (or name) the word as a noun or a verb. Writing a label on examples is a good way to remember something you have learned.

A. Read the paragraph. Write *N* (noun) or *V* (verb) above each bold word.

    I am a pilot. I like my **work**. I need to be very careful. The **result** of
                      N   2

bad decisions is sometimes terrible. My job is difficult, but the company

pays me very well. My job is also fun. I **travel** all over the world.

B. Is the bold word a noun or a verb? Check (✓) *Noun* or *Verb*.

	Noun	Verb
1. A doctor's **work** is never done.	☐	☐
2. My father **travels** to many countries for his company.	☐	☐
3. A good career for you **matches** your worker type.	☐	☐
4. A carpenter sees the **results** of his work every day.	☐	☐
5. What is your **plan** for your career?	☐	☐

 C. Go online for more practice with word forms.

WRITING

At the end of this unit you will write a few sentences about a job that is right for you. Your sentences will include specific information from the readings and your own ideas.

Writing Skill | Writing a main idea and supporting sentences

A **main idea** is the big idea. For example:

> My work is interesting.

Supporting sentences give more information about the main idea. For example:

> I meet new people.
> I learn about new products.

Supporting sentences give details about the main idea. Be sure the supporting sentences connect to the main idea. For example:

> Main idea: Construction workers need to be strong.
> They work with big machines.
> They lift heavy things.
> They wear warm clothes. [NOT a supporting sentence]

A. Match the supporting sentences to each main idea.

Sometimes they sleep in their trucks.
~~They answer customers' questions.~~
They explain new products.
They make new computer programs.
They think of new solutions to old problems.
They travel long distances.

---

1. Main idea: Sales assistants need to speak English well.

   Supporting sentence: _They answer customers' questions._

   Supporting sentence: _____

2. Main idea: Truck drivers are away from home many days a year.

Supporting sentence: _____

Supporting sentence: _____

3. Main idea: Software developers are creative people.

Supporting sentence: _____

Supporting sentence: _____

B. Cross out the one sentence that does not support the main idea.

1. Medical secretaries have many job duties.
   a. They answer the phone.
   b. They talk to patients about their records.
   c. They like science and technology.
   d. They schedule patients to see the doctor.

2. Accountants have many skills.
   a. They are good with numbers.
   b. They are well paid.
   c. They follow directions carefully.
   d. They are good with details.

3. Chefs work in many different types of kitchens.
   a. Some chefs work in hospital kitchens.
   b. Others work in restaurants or hotels.
   c. Some eat at home in their kitchens.
   d. Some cook in university or school kitchens.

4. Lawyers need many skills.
   a. They need to read, write, and speak very well.
   b. They need to work long hours.
   c. They need to make decisions quickly.
   d. They need to solve problems.

C. WRITING MODEL Underline the main idea in each model paragraph. Write SS at the beginning of each supporting sentence. Cross out the sentence that does not support the main idea.

1. Emergency Medical Technicians have many job responsibilities. ____ They drive an ambulance to an emergency. ____ They carry people to the ambulance. ____ They give people emergency medications. ____ They bring people to the hospital. ____ Their work is very important.

2. I want to be an Emergency Medical Technician. ____ I like to help people. ____ I like to make decisions and solve problems. ____ I want an exciting job. ____ Emergency Medical Technicians need to be strong. ____ I want to make a difference in people's lives.

Tip for Success

Remember to capitalize the first word in each sentence and end each sentence with a period.

D. Choose a sentence you wrote in your Quick Write on page 5. Copy the sentence. Then write three supporting sentences. For example:

Main idea:	I like to travel.
Supporting sentences:	I like to learn about new places.
	I like to meet new people.
	I like to try new foods.

 E. Go online for more practice with main ideas and supporting sentences.

Grammar Verbs + infinitives (*like*, *want*, and *need*)

Like, *want*, and *need* are common verbs. A noun or noun phrase or an infinitive form of a verb (*to* + base form of the verb) often follows *like*, *want*, or *need*.

Noun Phrase	Infinitive
I like **my career**.	I like **to help** people.
I want **a career**.	I want **to be** a doctor.
I need **a good job**.	I need **to work**.

A. Underline the noun phrases and circle the infinitives after the verbs *like*, *want*, and *need*.

1. I want (to be) a chef in a restaurant. I like (to work) with people. I like <u>good food</u>. I am creative.

2. I want to be an accountant. I like to solve problems in math. I like to work with details. I need good pay.

3. I want to be a truck driver. I like big trucks. I like to work alone. I want to see the country. I need to move around.

4. I want to be an office worker. I like regular hours. I like people. I need a job in an office.

B. Complete each sentence with your own ideas about jobs. Use a noun or a noun phrase and/or an infinitive with each verb.

1. I like _____.

2. I like _____.

3. I don't like _____.

4. I don't like _____.

5. I want _____.

6. I don't want _____.

7. I need _____.

8. I don't need _____.

C. Go online for more practice with verbs and infinitives.

D. Go online for the grammar expansion.

 In this assignment, you are going to write about a job you want. Describe the job responsibilities. Explain why the job is right for you. As you prepare to write, think about the Unit Question, "What is a good job?" Use information from Reading 1, Reading 2, the unit video, and your work in this unit to support your sentences. Refer to the Self-Assessment checklist on page 22.

 Go to the Online Writing Tutor for a writing model and alternate Unit Assignments.

PLAN AND WRITE

Tip for Success

You can learn about the duties of many jobs on the Internet. Search for *job duties* or *job description*.

A. **BRAINSTORM** Complete the activities.

1. List three interesting jobs. Then write three job responsibilities for each.

Job 1: _____

_____

Responsibility: _____

_____

Responsibility: _____

_____

Responsibility: _____

_____

Job 2: _____

_____

Responsibility: _____

_____

Responsibility: _____

_____

Responsibility: _____

_____

Job 3: _____

_____

Responsibility: _____

_____

Responsibility: _____

_____

Responsibility: _____

_____

2. What's important for you in a job? Check (✓) the things that are important. Add two more ideas to the list.

☐ good pay
☐ to help people
☐ to travel
☐ to work with people
☐ to work outside
☐ to work with numbers

☐ regular hours
☐ to see the results of my work
☐ to work alone
☐ to work in an office
☐ to work with details
☐ to work with my hands

☐ _____
☐ _____

B. PLAN Choose a job from your list in Activity A. Answer the questions.

1. What is a good job for you?

I want to be a(n) _____.

2. What are the duties of this job? Write the job and three job responsibilities.

A(n) _____ has three main responsibilities.

Responsibility 1: _____.

Responsibility 2: _____.

Responsibility 3: _____.

3. Why is it a good job for you? Write three reasons.

I like _____.

I want _____.

I need _____.

C. **WRITE** Use your **PLAN** notes to write sentences about a job you want. Go to *iQ Online* to use the Online Writing Tutor.

1. Make sure you have a main idea. Use supporting sentences to give more information about your main idea.

2. Look at the Self-Assessment checklist on page 22 to guide your writing.

REVISE AND EDIT

 A. **PEER REVIEW** Read your partner's sentences. Then go online and use the Peer Review worksheet. Discuss the review with your partner.

B. **REWRITE** Based on your partner's review, revise and rewrite your sentences.

C. **EDIT** Complete the Self-Assessment checklist as you prepare to write the final draft of your sentences. Be prepared to hand in your work or discuss it in class.

SELF-ASSESSMENT		
Yes	No	
☐	☐	Do you have a main idea?
☐	☐	Do the supporting sentences match the main idea?
☐	☐	Do you use the verbs *like*, *want*, and *need* correctly?
☐	☐	Does every sentence begin with a capital letter?
☐	☐	Does every sentence have final punctuation? (period, question mark)
☐	☐	Do your sentences include vocabulary from the unit?
☐	☐	Is the spelling correct? Check a dictionary if you are not sure.

 D. **REFLECT** Go to the Online Discussion Board to discuss these questions.

1. What is something new you learned in this unit?

2. Look back at the Unit Question—What is a good job? Is your answer different now than when you started the unit? If yes, how is it different? Why?

TRACK YOUR SUCCESS

Circle the words you have learned in this unit.

Nouns	Verbs	Adjectives
career 🔑	match 🔑	creative AWL
company 🔑	plan 🔑	flexible AWL
customer 🔑	solve 🔑	regular 🔑
decision 🔑		
event 🔑		
product 🔑		
result 🔑		
skill 🔑		
success 🔑		

🔑 Oxford 2000 keywords

AWL Academic Word List

Check (✓) the skills you learned. If you need more work on a skill, refer to the page(s) in parentheses.

READING	☐ I can preview a text. (p. 6)
VOCABULARY	☐ I can recognize and use words that are both nouns and verbs. (p. 15)
WRITING	☐ I can write a main idea and supporting sentences. (p. 16)
GRAMMAR	☐ I can recognize and use verbs + infinitives (*like*, *want*, and *need*). (p. 18)
UNIT OBJECTIVE ▶▶▶▶	☐ I can gather information and ideas to describe the duties of the job I want and give reasons that it is a good job for me.

READING ▶ skimming for the main idea
VOCABULARY ▶ word roots
WRITING ▶ writing compound sentences with *but* and *so*
GRAMMAR ▶ simple past with regular and irregular verbs

UNIT QUESTION

Why do people immigrate to other countries?

A Discuss these questions with your classmates.

1. Which countries in the world have a lot of immigrants?

2. Look at the photos. Do you think people today immigrate for the same reasons they did in the past?

B Listen to *The Q Classroom* online. Match the reasons in the box to the students. Do you agree or disagree? Check (✓) your answers in the chart below.

a. for education	c. to be with family
b. for job opportunities	d. for safety

	Reason	Agree	Disagree
Felix	b. for job opportunities	☐	☐
Yuna		☐	☐
Sophy		☐	☐
Marcus		☐	☐

iQ ONLINE **C** Go to the Online Discussion Board to discuss the Unit Question with your classmates.

D Look at the map of Europe with a partner. What do you know about these countries? Try to say one thing about each country.

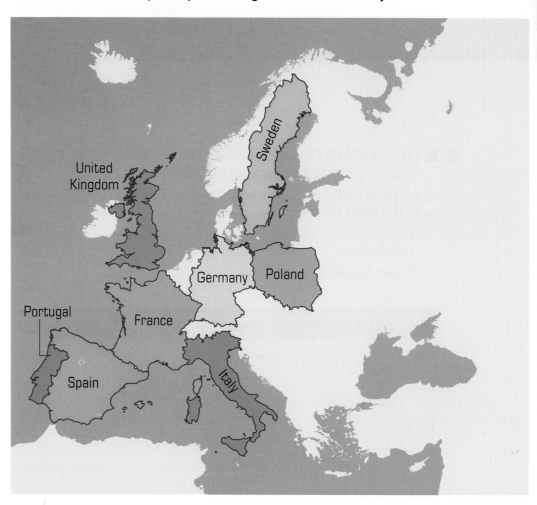

E Write the names of six other countries you know. Work with a partner. If possible, add the countries to the map.

_____   _____   _____

_____   _____   _____

F Answer the questions with your partner.

1. Do you know people from other countries? Which countries?

2. Do you sometimes travel to other countries? Which countries do you visit?

READING

UNIT OBJECTIVE ▶▶▶▶

You are going to read a Web page about London. Use the Web page to gather information and ideas for your Unit Assignment.

PREVIEW THE READING

Vocabulary Skill Review

Pay attention to the part of speech information in each definition. As you do Activity A, think about which part of speech is needed in each sentence. Does the sentence need a verb, a noun, or an adjective?

A. VOCABULARY Here are some words from Reading 1. Read their definitions. Then complete each sentence.

> **celebrate** *(verb)* 🔑 to do something special on an important day
>
> **international** *(adjective)* 🔑 between different countries
>
> **market** *(noun)* 🔑 a place where people go to buy and sell things, usually outside
>
> **million** *(number)* 🔑 1,000,000
>
> **neighborhood** *(noun)* a part of a town or city; the people who live there
>
> **population** *(noun)* the number of people who live in a place
>
> **sights** *(noun)* 🔑 interesting places to see

🔑 Oxford 2000 keywords

1. Many people buy vegetables and fruits at their local _____.

2. People from many different countries live and work in New York City. It is an _____ city.

3. Riyadh is a very large city. About 5 _____ people live there.

4. People in this country don't have many children. The _____ is going down.

5. I want to live in this _____. The houses and schools are very nice.

6. We _____ the new year with special food and fireworks.

7. There are many famous _____ to see in London, like the Tower of London.

B. Go online for more practice with the vocabulary.

C. **PREVIEW** Look at the title, headings, pictures, and captions. What does the Web page say about London? Check (✓) the answer.

☐ London is fun for families.

☐ People in London come from many different countries.

☐ People from London like to visit many countries.

D. **QUICK WRITE** An international city is a city where people from many countries live and work. What international cities do you know? Who lives in these cities? Write a few sentences. Remember to use this section for your Unit Assignment.

WORK WITH THE READING

A. Read the Web page and gather information about why people immigrate to other countries.

The World in a City

London

1   Do you plan to visit London? There are many English **sights** to see, but there are many **international** sights, sounds, and foods, too. London is a city with many different groups of people. In a visit to London, you see the world.

Population

2   The **population** of the city of London is about eight **million**. Over three million of these people are from **other** countries. In London, you can hear over 300 languages spoken.

Eat

3   There is food from more than 55 different countries in London's restaurants. There is even food from countries such as Tanzania, Peru, and Mongolia. At food **markets**, you can buy vegetables and fruits from all over the world.

A street in London

The following are the top ten countries of birth[1] for today's immigrants in London:

1. India	6. Sri Lanka
2. Poland	7. Jamaica
3. Bangladesh	8. Pakistan
4. Nigeria	9. South Africa
5. Ireland	10. Germany

[1] **country of birth:** the country a person is born in

Visit

4   People from many countries live and work in the **neighborhoods** of London. You can go to the neighborhoods to see interesting people, shops, restaurants, and events from all over the world. London also has more than 240 museums! Go to the museums to see old and new art from many different countries.

Celebrate

5   London has many international festivals with food, music, art, and dance. In winter, you can **celebrate** Chinese New Year. In early spring, you can celebrate the Russian end of winter. In the summer, you can go to the largest Caribbean festival in the world. In the fall, you can enjoy the Indian festival of lights.

London's food markets have fruits and vegetables from all over the world.

London has many festivals all year long.

Tip for Success

Read a text two times or more. The first time, read for the main ideas. Then read it again for details.

B. According to the Web page, what are five activities that you can do to see the world in London?

☐ Eat in a restaurant.   ☐ Read the newspapers.

☐ Go to a food market.   ☐ Go to museums.

☐ Ride a bus.   ☐ Visit the neighborhoods.

☐ Go to a festival.

C. Read the statements. Check (✓) true or false. Then correct each false statement to make it true.

1. About three million people live in London.   ☐ True   ☐ False

    _____

    _____

2. About one million Londoners were born outside of England.   ☐ True   ☐ False

    _____

    _____

3. People in London speak over 300 languages.   ☐ True   ☐ False

_____

_____

4. There is food from more than 65 countries in
London's restaurants.   ☐ True   ☐ False

_____

_____

5. Poland is the number 1 country of birth of today's
London immigrants.   ☐ True   ☐ False

_____

_____

6. In London museums you can see things from all over   ☐ True   ☐ False
the world.

_____

_____

**D. Where is this information on the Web page? Write the correct paragraph
number next to each statement.**

____ London is a city with many things to see.

____ There is food from all around the world in London.

____ There are great neighborhoods in London.

____ There are interesting festivals all year long.

____ The people in London come from many countries.

____ London has many museums.

E. What did you learn about London in Reading 1? Write one sentence in your own words about each topic.

1. People: _____

2. Food: _____

3. Neighborhoods: _____

4. Festivals: _____

WRITE WHAT YOU THINK

A. Think about your city or town. How international is it? Are there international restaurants and festivals? Are there international museums? Do people from different countries live in your city or town?

B. Think about the immigrants in your city or town. Where are they from? What neighborhoods do they live in? What do you know about the immigrants in your area?

C. Choose the questions from A or B and write a response. Look back at your Quick Write on page 28 as you think about what you have learned.

Question: _____

My response: _____

_____

_____

_____

READING 2 | Immigrant Stories

You are going to read a magazine article that tells the stories of three immigrants. Use the article to gather information and ideas for your Unit Assignment.

PREVIEW THE READING

A. **VOCABULARY** Here are some words from Reading 2. Read the sentences. Then write each <u>underlined</u> word next to the correct definition.

1. I'm so excited. I have the <u>opportunity</u> to go to London this year.

2. John doesn't have any friends. He is <u>lonely</u>.

3. I work in a restaurant now, but I want to have my <u>own</u> restaurant.

4. Children need their parents to <u>support</u> them. They need food, money, love, and many other things.

5. One year is not enough. You need <u>several</u> years to make a new life in a new country.

6. Many people from Jamaica live in London. They have a large <u>community</u> there.

a. _____ (*noun*) a group of people who are together, for example, because they have the same interests or background

b. _____ (*verb*) to help someone to live by giving them things like money, a home, or food

c. _____ (*adjective*) unhappy because you are not with other people

d. _____ (*adjective*) belonging to a particular person

e. _____ (*noun*) a chance to do something

f. _____ (*adjective*) more than two but not many

 B. Go online for more practice with the vocabulary.

🔑 Oxford 2000 keywords

Skimming is reading a text quickly to find the main idea. People often skim articles online, in newspapers, or in magazines. They look quickly at all sections of the article to get the main idea. Then they decide if they want to take more time to read the article carefully.

Skimming is useful when you want to get a quick idea of the reading.

Here are some tips to help you skim for the main idea.

- Read the title.

- Read the headings of each section.

- Read the first and last sentences of each paragraph. Often the main idea is at the beginning or end of a paragraph.

C. PREVIEW **Skim the article. Then write *T* (true) and *F* (false) for each statement.**

____ 1. The three immigrants are from different countries.

____ 2. The three immigrants all live in England.

____ 3. The three immigrants are students.

  D. Go online for more practice with skimming.

E. QUICK WRITE **What problems do immigrants have when they change countries? What things can be better? Write a few sentences. Remember to use this section for your Unit Assignment.**

WORK WITH THE READING

A. Read the article and gather information about why people immigrate to other countries.

Immigrant Stories

1   Immigrants in London—Why are they in London? Are they happy to live here? Do they plan to stay? Read their stories and find the answers!

Story 1: Sun Yun Wing

2   My name is Sun Yun Wing. I am from a small town near Hong Kong. In 1965, there weren't many

Sun Yun Wing

jobs there. There were many job **opportunities** in England, so I came to London. I was 20 years old.

3   I had many problems at first. I didn't speak English. The weather was cold and rainy. I was **lonely** because my family didn't come with me, but there were good things about living in London. There were many jobs with good pay.

4   I got my first job in a Chinese restaurant. Now, I have my **own** restaurant. I work there with my wife. She is also Chinese. Her English is good, so she speaks to the customers. I am the chef. We work very hard.

5   We have three children. They have good jobs. They do not want to live in Hong Kong. My wife and I don't know anyone in Hong Kong now. Our life is here. This is our home.

Story 2: Basher Ali

6   My name is Basher Ali. I am from a small town in Bangladesh. I came to England in 1985 with my wife and two small children. I was 25 years old. I immigrated to England to give my family a better life.

7   My first job in England was in a factory[1]. At night, I went to school. I studied English and business on nights and weekends.

8   Now, I have my own business. I sell clothing from Bangladesh. My business is very successful. I have **several** clothing stores.

[1] **factory:** a place where people make things, usually with machines

9   I try to help my people. In London, I give English classes at my stores for the Bangladeshi **community**. I send money to my relatives and my town in Bangladesh. I **support** a children's language school there.

10   I have good children. They work in my company. They keep Bangladeshi ways in their families. They are successful in England, but they are still Bangladeshi in their hearts.

Story 3: Apara Asuquo

11   My name is Apara Asuquo. I am from Lagos, Nigeria. I came to London in 2008 with my husband. I was 45 years old. My husband works for an **international** bank here in London. He worked in an office of the same bank in Nigeria. We moved here for his career.

12   I was a successful businesswoman[2] in my country, but I had no success finding a job here in London. After two years, my husband said, "This is a different country. This is your new life. You need to start from the beginning

Apara Asuquo

again." So I got a job as an office worker. The pay isn't very good, but I like the people.

13   Our children go to university in England. My husband and I plan to return to Nigeria, but our children plan to stay here. They have many opportunities here. It is always sad to say goodbye, but for my husband and me, Nigeria is our home.

---

[2] **businesswoman:** a woman who works in business, especially in a top position

B. Circle the answer to each question.

Sun Yun Wing

1. Is he happy living in England?   Yes   No

2. Does he plan to stay?   Yes   No

Basher Ali

3. Is he happy living in England?   Yes   No

4. Does he plan to stay?   Yes   No

Apara Asuquo

5. Is she happy living in England?   Yes   No

6. Does she plan to stay?   Yes   No

C. **What do we know about each person?**

1. What do we know about Sun Yun Wing?
   - ☐ He is from Hong Kong.
   - ☐ He came to London alone.
   - ☐ He is married.
   - ☐ He went to school in Hong Kong.
   - ☐ He is a grandfather.

2. What do we know about Basher Ali?
   - ☐ He is from a small town in Bangladesh.
   - ☐ He came to London with his family.
   - ☐ He learned English in school in London.
   - ☐ He goes back to Bangladesh often.
   - ☐ He is a grandfather.

3. What do we know about Apara Asuquo?
   - ☐ She is from a big city.
   - ☐ She has five children.
   - ☐ She was successful in Nigeria.
   - ☐ She came with her husband.
   - ☐ She misses Nigeria.

D. **Read the stories again. Check (✓) the problems and successes of each immigrant. You may check more than one person for each statement.**

	Sun Yun Wing	Basher Ali	Apara Asuquo
1. I was lonely.	☐	☐	☐
2. I didn't find a good job.	☐	☐	☐
3. There were no good jobs.	☐	☐	☐
4. I was sad without my family.	☐	☐	☐
5. I have a business in England.	☐	☐	☐
6. I help my community.	☐	☐	☐
7. My children go to university in England.	☐	☐	☐
8. My children have good jobs.	☐	☐	☐

E. What do you think? Circle your answer. Find an example from the article to support your answer.

1. Is it better to immigrate when you are young?   Yes   No

Example from the reading: _____

2. Is it easier to immigrate with family?   Yes   No

Example from the reading: _____

3. Is it important to learn the language of the new country?   Yes   No

Example from the reading: _____

F. Look back at your Quick Write on page 33. Add new information you learned from the reading. Have any of your answers changed?

 G. Go online to read *Living In Tokyo* and check your comprehension.

 # WRITE WHAT YOU THINK

A. Discuss the questions in a group. Look back at your Quick Write on page 33 as you think about what you learned.

1. In Activity D on page 36, numbers 1–4 tell about problems immigrants have in London. What problems do immigrants have where you live?

2. In Activity D on page 36, numbers 5–8 tell about successes London immigrants have. What are the successes of immigrants where you live?

 B. Go online to watch the video about how one immigrant gives to his community. Then check your comprehension.

> **community groups** (n.) groups in a community, like children's sports teams, arts organizations, or book groups
> **fundraiser** (n.) an event that makes money for a group
> **volunteer** (v.) to work for free to help a group or a cause

VIDEO VOCABULARY

C. Think about the unit video, Reading 1, and Reading 2 as you discuss the questions. Then choose one question and write a response.

1. Is immigration good for countries like England?

2. How do immigrants help a country?

3. What are some problems with immigration?

The **root** of a word is the part of a word with the basic meaning.

> lone   alone
>
> lonely   loneliness

The root is *lone*, which means "without another person." The meaning of each of the words relates to this basic meaning. Learning roots can increase your vocabulary and help you guess the meaning of a new word in a text.

A. These words from the unit have word roots (in bold). Match each word root with its definition.

> **fac**tory   im**migra**te   inter**nat**ional   **pop**ulation

Word Roots	Definitions
____ 1. nat	a. people
____ 2. pop	b. to do or make
____ 3. fac	c. to be born or come from
____ 4. migra	d. to move

B. Here are more words with the same roots. Match each word with its definition.

Words	Definitions
____ 1. emigrate	a. belonging to a place from birth
____ 2. native	b. to fill an area with people
____ 3. populate	c. to make things using machines
____ 4. manufacture	d. to leave your country for another country

 C. Go online for more practice with word roots.

WRITING

At the end of this unit you will write about a place that changed with immigration. Your sentences will include specific information from the readings and your own ideas.

Writing Skill Writing compound sentences with *but* and *so*

You can connect two simple sentences with *but* to give opposite or different information. Use a comma before *but*.

> She is happy, **but** she misses home.
> She likes the English language, **but** she doesn't like English weather.

You can connect two simple sentences with *so* when the second sentence is a result of the first sentence. Use a comma before *so*.

> There were no jobs in his country, **so** he immigrated to the United States.
> His doesn't speak English well, **so** he goes to English classes.

A. Complete each sentence with *but* or *so*.

1. She wanted to help her family back home, _____ she sent money every month.

2. He was a teacher in his native country, _____ he isn't a teacher in the United States.

3. There are great opportunities for immigrants, _____ there are also many problems.

4. There are many Indian immigrants in London, _____ there are many Indian restaurants in London.

5. London is an English city, _____ it is an international city, too.

6. He went to school in London, _____ he can speak English very well.

B. Read the sentences. Connect them with *but* or *so*. Remember to use commas.

1. There were no jobs in his small town.
   He moved to a big city.

   <u>There were no jobs in his small town, so he moved to a big city.</u>

2. She had good business skills.
She did not get a job.

_____

3. People speak many different languages in London.
Most people speak English.

_____

4. His family didn't come with him.
He was very lonely.

_____

5. She was a doctor in Colombia.
She is a medical secretary here.

_____

6. Many people from the Caribbean live in London.
London has very big Caribbean festivals.

_____

C. Complete the sentences. Use information about yourself.

1. I want to learn English, so I _____ .

2. I want to learn English, but I _____ .

 D. Go online for more practice writing compound sentences with _but_ and _so_.

| Grammar | Simple past with regular and irregular verbs |

Regular verbs

Use the **simple past** to talk about actions that happened in the past.

- To form the simple past of regular verbs, add -_ed_ to the base form of the verb.

  _He_ work**ed** _in a factory._

- For verbs ending in _e_, just add -_d_.

  They mov**ed** _to London in 2013._

- For verbs ending in _y_, drop the _y_ and add -_ied_.

  She stud**ied** _English in school._

Irregular verbs

Past of *be*

- The verb *be* is irregular in the simple past. It has two forms: *was* and *were*. Use *was* with *I, he, she,* and *it.* Use *were* with *we, you,* and *they.*

   I **was** in London.
   You **were** in the neighborhood.
   She **was** new to the country.
   He **was** a good student.
   It **was** cold.
   We **were** at the museum.
   They **were** from China.

- Here are some common irregular verbs with their simple past forms.

buy	**bought**		know	**knew**
come	**came**		make	**made**
do	**did**		say	**said**
get	**got**		speak	**spoke**
go	**went**		take	**took**
have	**had**			

Negative forms of the simple past

- To form a negative statement, use *did + not* (or *didn't*) + base form of the verb.

   We **didn't work** nights. We worked days.
   I **didn't go** home for dinner. I went to a restaurant.
   She **didn't speak** English. She spoke Tagalog.

A. Look back at Reading 2 on pages 34 and 35. Circle all the verbs in the reading about Basher Ali. Write the verbs in the correct column of the chart below.

Present	Past

B. Complete each sentence with the past tense of *be*.

1. I _____ sad to say goodbye.

2. You _____ successful in your job.

3. She _____ happy to start a new life.

4. It _____ a small town.

5. Sami _____ ready to try something new.

6. We _____ able to find work.

7. You and I _____ at our jobs morning and night.

8. Kim and Sun _____ happy to speak Korean together.

C. Complete each sentence with the simple past form of the verb in parentheses.

1. New York City is an old city of immigrants. The Dutch
_____ the land from the Native Americans in 1626.
    (buy)

2. In the mid 1800's many people from Germany and Ireland
_____ to New York City.
    (move)

3. In 1880, 12,000 Italians _____ in New York City.
    (live)

4. Over the next thirty years, many Italians _____ to New
    (come)
York City.

5. In 1910, 341,000 Italians _____ in New York City.
    (be)

6. Nearly a million immigrants _____ New York City their
    (make)
home between 1990 and 2000.

7. One third of the immigrants _____ from Latin America.
    (arrive)

8. In 2005 more than half of the people in New York City were immigrants
or _____ immigrant parents.
    (have)

D. Go online for more practice with the simple past.

E. Go online for the grammar expansion.

In this assignment, you are going to write about a place that changed because of international immigration or international culture. As you prepare to write, think about the Unit Question, "Why do people immigrate to other countries?" Use information from Reading 1, Reading 2, the unit video, and your work in this unit to support your writing. Refer to the Self-Assessment checklist on page 44.

Go to the Online Writing Tutor for a writing model and alternate Unit Assignments.

PLAN AND WRITE

A. BRAINSTORM Complete the activities.

1. Think about a place that changed because of immigration. Write the name of the place.

2. How did immigration or international culture change this place? Think about the place now and in the past. What are some changes in businesses, restaurants, supermarkets, languages people speak, schools, and families? Also remember changes you read about in this unit.

B. PLAN Complete the chart with information about the neighborhood, town, or city from Exercise A.

	Past	Today
People Where were the people from? Where are they from today?		
Foods What food was available? What food is available today?		
Culture What music, art, and festivals were common? What music, art, and festivals are common today?		
Business What kinds of business, shops, and markets were there? What kinds are there today?		

C. WRITE Use your PLAN notes to write your sentences. Go to *iQ Online* to use the Online Writing Tutor.

1. Use your information from Exercises A and B. Try to include some compound sentences with *but* and *so*.

2. Look at the Self-Assessment checklist to guide your writing.

REVISE AND EDIT

A. PEER REVIEW Read your partner's sentences. Then go online and use the Peer Review worksheet. Discuss the review with your partner.

B. REWRITE Based on your partner's review, revise and rewrite your sentences.

C. EDIT Complete the Self-Assessment checklist as you prepare to write the final draft of your sentences. Be prepared to hand in your work or discuss it in class.

SELF-ASSESSMENT		
Yes	No	
☐	☐	Do you have a main idea?
☐	☐	Do all your sentences support your main idea?
☐	☐	Do you use both simple sentences and compound sentences connected with *but* or *so*?
☐	☐	Do you have verbs in the simple past? Are the verbs spelled correctly?
☐	☐	Do your sentences include vocabulary from the unit?
☐	☐	Is the spelling correct? Check a dictionary if you are not sure.
☐	☐	Does every sentence begin with a capital letter?
☐	☐	Does every sentence have final punctuation? (period, question mark)

D. REFLECT Go to the Online Discussion Board to discuss these questions.

1. What is something new you learned in this unit?

2. Look back at the Unit Question—Why do people immigrate to other countries? Is your answer different now than when you started the unit? If yes, how is it different? Why?

TRACK YOUR SUCCESS

Circle the words you have learned in this unit.

Nouns
community 🔑 AWL
market 🔑
neighborhood
opportunity 🔑
population
sights 🔑

Verbs
celebrate 🔑
support 🔑

Numbers
million 🔑

Adjectives
international 🔑
lonely 🔑
own 🔑
several 🔑

🔑 Oxford 2000 keywords
AWL Academic Word List

Check (✓) the skills you learned. If you need more work on a skill, refer to the page(s) in parentheses.

READING ■	I can skim for the main idea. (p. 33)
VOCABULARY ■	I can recognize word roots. (p. 38)
WRITING ■	I can connect sentences with *but* and *so*. (p. 39)
GRAMMAR ■	I can recognize and use the simple past. (p. 40)
UNIT OBJECTIVE ▶▶▶	■ I can gather information and ideas to explain how a place changed because of international immigration or culture.

UNIT 3

Sociology

READING	▶	reading charts, graphs, and tables
VOCABULARY	▶	modifying nouns
WRITING	▶	using correct paragraph structure
GRAMMAR	▶	sentences with *because*

UNIT QUESTION

Why is vacation important?

A Discuss these questions with your classmates.

1. How much vacation do you get? Which jobs give more vacation? Which jobs give less?

2. Look at the photo. Is this a vacation you would take? Why or why not?

B Listen to *The Q Classroom* online. Then answer these questions.

1. Sophy says that we work hard when we come back from vacation. Why?

2. Marcus says that vacation makes people healthier. Why?

3. Felix says that vacation is a time to make important decisions. Why?

 C Go to the Online Discussion Board to discuss the Unit Question with your classmates.

D Work with a partner. Look at the photos. Which vacation activities do you like best? Take turns telling your partner about your favorite activities.

going to the beach

hiking in the mountains

visiting famous places

visiting theme parks

E Complete the chart for yourself and a partner.

	Me	My Partner
1. How often do you take a vacation?		
2. How long is your vacation usually?		
3. What do you do on vacation?		
4. Who do you go on vacation with?		

READING 1 | Vacation Policy

You are going to read an email about a vacation policy at a business. Use the email to gather information and ideas for your Unit Assignment.

PREVIEW THE READING

A. VOCABULARY Here are some words from Reading 1. Read the paragraphs. Then write each underlined word next to the correct definition.

wooden toys

Toys Inc. is a small toy company. It <u>produces</u> beautiful wooden toys. There are 36 <u>employees</u> at Toys Inc. Most of the employees have special woodworking skills.

Toys Inc. <u>competes</u> with many other toy companies. Some times of year are very busy, and the employees work very long hours. They work an <u>average</u> of 50 hours a week. Recently, several employees left the company. They left because they were stressed by the long hours.

The company president wants to <u>improve</u> employees' experience at work. She believes employees are <u>likely</u> to work better when they take time to <u>rest</u> and relax. The president will write a new vacation <u>policy</u> so that more Toys Inc. employees take vacation from work.

1. _____ *(verb)* to make or grow something

2. _____ *(verb)* to relax, to sleep, to do nothing

3. _____ *(verb)* to try to do something better than someone else

4. _____ *(verb)* to become better or to make something better

5. _____ *(noun)* people who work for someone else

6. _____ *(noun)* the plans of a government, organization, or company

7. _____ *(adjective)* probably

8. _____ *(noun)* the normal or usual amount

 B. Go online for more practice with the vocabulary.

C. **PREVIEW** Skim the email header. Answer the questions.

1. Who is the email from?

   _____

2. Who is the email to?

   _____

3. What is the email about?

   _____

D. **QUICK WRITE** What do you know about vacation policies? Write a few sentences. Remember to use this section for your Unit Assignment.

WORK WITH THE READING

A. Read the email and gather information about why vacation is important.

Tip for Success

Underline the most important information in a reading text. After you read the text, study the parts you underlined. This helps you remember the information in the text.

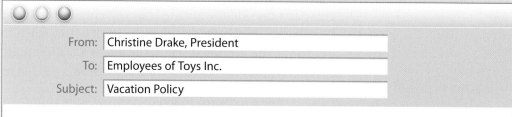

From: Christine Drake, President
To: Employees of Toys Inc.
Subject: Vacation Policy

At Toys Inc. we want you to be happy, healthy, and successful **employees**. We know you work hard, and we believe vacations are the best way for you to **rest** and relax. Many of you, however, do not use all your vacation days. Some of you don't take vacation at all! This year employees used an **average** of only four vacation days.

Not taking vacation hurts you and the company.

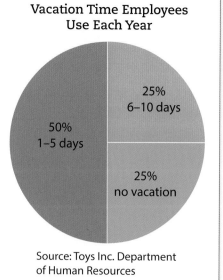

Vacation Time Employees Use Each Year

25% 6–10 days

50% 1–5 days

25% no vacation

Source: Toys Inc. Department of Human Resources

Tired employees are more **likely** to have accidents and get hurt. Tired employees are more likely to feel stress and get sick. Every time an employee gets hurt or sick, we **produce** less. Every time a person gets hurt or sick, your co-workers need to work harder to do your work, too.

Tired employees are more likely to be unhappy and leave the job. You are very skilled woodworkers. We don't want to lose you!

Vacations **improve** the work you do. You have more energy. You produce more. Vacations are good for business because they are good for employees.

Next year we will start a new vacation **policy** because you need to take your vacations. We want to know which policy works best for you. Please read about the two policies. Then check (✓) the one you like best. Please return your email with your choice by the end of the day Friday. I will decide on the policy after I hear from you.

☐ **Policy A: Close the company for two weeks every year.**

With Policy A, we close our business for two weeks every year: one week in the summer and one week in the winter. All employees take their vacation during those two weeks. Many companies around the world have this policy.

Reasons for and against Policy A:

Many employees go on vacation, but they don't stop thinking about work. They call the company during their vacation. They check the company email. Closing the company solves this problem. Everyone gets a real vacation.

The big summer and winter holidays already slow down business. Many employees take vacation around the holidays. This means half the employees are away, and the other half are working too hard. By closing the doors, everyone takes time to relax.

This policy does have a problem. Toys Inc. is number 1 in wooden toys. We might lose business if we close for two weeks. It will be difficult to **compete** if we close our doors.

☐ **Policy B: Use your vacation days or lose them.**

In Policy B, employees need to use their 10 vacation days each year. If you do not use the days, you lose the days. You cannot save the days and use them the next year. Many companies now have this vacation policy.

Reasons for and against Policy B:

Employees can decide when to use the vacation days. You can plan a vacation around your family's work and school schedules.

Many employees like to take several short vacations during the year. This policy lets you take a couple of days off now and then to take short vacations.

This policy works well for the company. However, when employees take vacations at different times, their co-workers need to work harder to do the extra work. This creates stress for employees who are not on vacation.

B. Which policy do these statements describe: A or B? Check (✓) the correct box.

	Policy A	Policy B
1. Employees take their vacation any time.		
2. Employees take their vacation at the same time.		
3. The company closes for two weeks a year.		
4. The company stays open all year long.		

C. Write the letter of the answer that best completes each statement.

1. Several employees left Toys Inc. ___.

    a. because employees were not taking vacation.

2. Toys Inc. is starting a new vacation policy ___.

    b. because happy employees produce more.

3. Tired employees produce less ___.

    c. because they get sick more often.

4. Vacations are good for business ___.

    d. because they were stressed and tired.

D. Complete the chart with reasons for and against each policy. Use information from the Reading.

> all employees get a real vacation
> difficult to compete with other companies
> flexible vacation time
> more co-worker stress
> no one calls into work while on vacation
> several short vacations

Reasons for Policy A	Reason Against Policy A

Reasons for Policy B	Reason Against Policy B

E. Look back at your Quick Write on page 50. Add new information about vacation policies that you learned from the reading.

Many texts you read have **charts**, **graphs**, or **tables** in them. Charts, graphs, and tables are very useful because they give a lot of information in a small space. They also make it easier to understand a text.

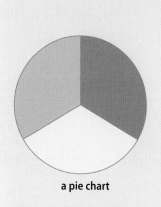

a pie chart

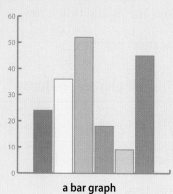

a bar graph

	XXXXX	XXXXX
1		
2		
3		
4		

a table

It's important to look at charts, graphs, and tables when you *preview* and *skim*, a text. Here are some tips.

- Read the title and headings to get the main idea.
- Look at the numbers. To find details, scan for only the numbers that you want to know about.

A. Look at the pie chart in Reading 1 on page 50. Answer the questions.

1. What is the title? _____

2. What percentage of employees at Toys Inc. take 1–5 vacation days?

_____

3. What percentage of employees at Toys Inc. do not take any vacation?

_____

B. Look at the table and answer the questions below.

Critical Thinking **Tip**

Activities A, B, and C ask you to **interpret** a table or a graph. To interpret, you have to take information in one form and change it into another form. In these activities, you have to use numbers to understand ideas.

Vacation Days per Year			
	Average Number of Vacation Days Employers Give	Average Number of Vacation Days Employees Take	Average Number of Vacation Days Employees Do Not Use
Brazil	30	30	0
France	30	30	0
Japan	18	7	11
Malaysia	17	14	3
Mexico	12	10	2
United Kingdom	25	25	0
United States	14	10	4

1. What is the title of the table? _____

2. In which countries do people take the most vacation? _____

   and _____

3. How many vacation days do employers give in the United States?

   _____

4. How many vacation days do people take in the United States?

   _____

5. How many vacation days do employers give in the United Kingdom?

   _____

6. How many days of vacation do employees take in the United Kingdom?

   _____

7. What do you think? Why don't people in the United States, Mexico, and Japan take all their vacation days?

_____

8. What do you think? Why do people in Brazil and France take all their vacation days?

_____

C. Look at the bar graph and answer the questions.

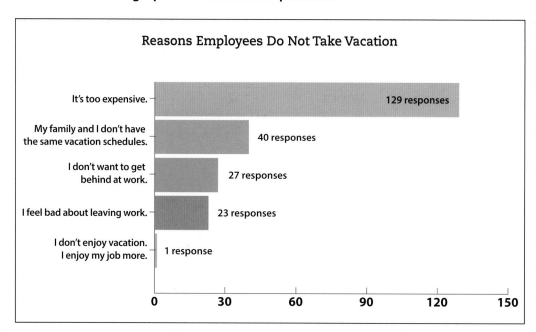

Reasons Employees Do Not Take Vacation

It's too expensive.	129 responses
My family and I don't have the same vacation schedules.	40 responses
I don't want to get behind at work.	27 responses
I feel bad about leaving work.	23 responses
I don't enjoy vacation. I enjoy my job more.	1 response

(0   30   60   90   120   150)

1. What is the title? _____

2. What is the number-one reason people do not take vacation?

_____

3. How many people don't enjoy vacation? _____

4. How many people cannot take vacation at the same time as their

family? _____

 D. Go online for more practice reading charts, graphs, and tables.

WRITE WHAT YOU THINK

A. Discuss the questions in a group.

1. The President of Toys Inc. wants employees to take vacations. How do the two policies get employees to use their vacation time? What are other ways to get employees to use their vacation time?

2. Are vacations the only way to rest and relax? What are other ways employees can rest and relax?

B. Choose one of the questions from Exercise A and write a response. Look back at your Quick Write on page 50 as you think about what you learned.

Question: ____

My response: _____

_____

_____

_____

READING 2 | Managing Life and Work with Dr. Sanders

UNIT OBJECTIVE ▶▶▶▶ You are going to read a blog post about vacations. Use the blog to gather information and ideas for your Unit Assignment.

PREVIEW THE READING

Vocabulary Skill Review

In Unit 2, you learned about word roots. The root of the word *benefits* is *bene*. Use a dictionary to find the meaning of *bene*. What are some other words with the same root?

A. **VOCABULARY** Here are some words from Reading 2. Read the sentences. Circle the answer that best matches the meaning of each **underlined** word.

1. In the summer I travel <u>abroad</u> to learn new languages and try new experiences.
   a. to other countries
   b. in my country

2. She has a good <u>attitude</u> about work. She believes work is important but it is not everything.
   a. way of thinking
   b. way of reading

3. Exercise has many <u>benefits</u>. You lose weight and get healthy.
   a. bad results
   b. good results

Oxford 2000 keywords

4. If you pay attention, you can <u>discover</u> new things every day.
   a. forget about
   b. learn about

5. His trip to Turkey was a <u>positive</u> experience. He was happy he went.
   a. bad
   b. good

6. On vacations, I <u>connect</u> with my family. We have fun together.
   a. feel close to
   b. feel distant from

7. People come back from vacation more relaxed. Vacations <u>reduce</u> stress.
   a. increase
   b. lower

B. Go online for more practice with the vocabulary.

C. **PREVIEW** Look at the headings in the blog and answer the questions.

1. Who writes the blog? _____

2. What is the name of the blog? _____

3. What is the title of this blog post? _____

D. **QUICK WRITE** What are the benefits of a short vacation? What are the benefits of a long vacation? Write a few sentences. Remember to use this section for your Unit Assignment.

WORK WITH THE READING

A. Read the article and gather information about why vacation is important.

Managing Life and Work with Dr. Sanders

Is a short vacation better than a long one?

1   We all know vacations are good for our health. Indeed, regular vacations **reduce** heart attacks in men by 30% and in women by 50%. But which kind of vacation is better: one long vacation, or several short ones?

2   Here is information from research studies. Read about the **benefits** of each kind of vacation. Then decide which kind of vacation is best for you.

Oxford 2000 keywords

The Benefits of a Long Vacation

3   International travel makes a vacation longer, but the benefits are big. Several studies show that people who spend their vacations **abroad** are more creative when they come back home. When people spend time in other countries, they **discover** different ways people live. This results in more creative thinking and better problem solving.

4   Many studies show that people do not get good quality sleep until day two or three of their vacation. After day two or day three, they continue to sleep well for the whole vacation. They also sleep well for one week after vacation. A long vacation means better sleep for more days.

5   Traveling on vacation can be stressful. It takes time and money to travel. If you spend more time on your vacation, you get more days of relaxation for your days of travel stress.

6   If there is a problem at work, and you are away on a long vacation, your co-workers are more likely to take care of the problem. They are not likely to wait for you to come back from vacation. The result? You have less work waiting for you when you get back to work.

The Benefits of Short Vacations

7   Several studies discovered that people enjoy planning for their vacation as much as they enjoy taking the vacation. If you plan four short vacations a year, you can experience the fun of planning the vacation four different times in one year.

8   Many people do NOT call the office when they are away on a short vacation. People on long vacations are more likely to check email and worry about work. For example, France has the highest number of vacation days (30 days a year), and also the highest number of vacationers who check their work email (93%).

9   Vacations improve our **attitude** about our lives, our families, and ourselves. When we get back to work, we quickly forget all those **positive** feelings. Taking several short vacations a year helps you feel positive about your life more often.

10   We all have very busy lives. Family, school, and work schedules are full. It is difficult to find a whole week when everyone can go on vacation. A short vacation is easier to fit in to our busy schedules. The busier we are, the more important it is to **connect** with friends and family on vacation.

B. What is the main idea of the blog? Check (✓) one.

☐ Short vacations are better than long vacations.

☐ Long vacations are better than short vacations.

☐ Short and long vacations have different benefits.

☐ All vacations have the same benefits.

C. Which statements support short vacations? Which statements support long vacations? Write *S* (short) or *L* (long) next to each statement.

___ 1. People enjoy planning vacations as much as they enjoy taking vacations.

___ 2. Traveling abroad makes a person more creative.

___ 3. People on long vacations call in to work more often.

___ 4. People quickly lose the benefits of vacation.

___ 5. Families have very busy schedules.

___ 6. Co-workers take care of problems at work when an employee is away for several weeks.

___ 7. It takes a few days of relaxation to improve sleep quality.

___ 8. Travel has benefits, but it is stressful.

People quickly lose the benefits of vacation.

D. Which do you prefer, long or short vacations? Why? Choose one reason from the article to support your answer.

_____

_____

_____

E. Look back at your Quick Write on page 58. Add anything you learned about the benefits of taking vacations.

F. Go online to read *Tourism in France* and check your comprehension.

WRITE WHAT YOU THINK

A. Discuss the questions in a group. Look back at your Quick Write on page 58 as you think about what you learned.

1. The blog talks about the benefits of taking a vacation. What benefits do you hope for when you take a vacation? Circle 3 and discuss your choices.

   a. discover new places
   b. get better sleep
   c. connect with family
   d. reduce heart attacks
   e. feel good about yourself and your life
   f. get away from work or school

2. What is your idea of a great vacation? Where do you want to go? What do you want to do?

B. Go online to watch the video about children and summer school. Then check your comprehension.

Writing Tip

Remember to support your main idea with several supporting sentences.

C. Think about the unit video, Reading 1, and Reading 2 as you discuss the questions. Then choose one question and write a response.

1. What is better for children: one long vacation or several short vacations? Why?

2. Do you think people should take more vacations? Why or why not?

Question: _____

My response: _____

_____

_____

_____

We often put two nouns together to form a **modifying noun**. The first noun describes the second noun. It acts like an adjective.

> classroom time = time in a classroom
> family needs = needs of a family
> summer vacation = vacation during the summer

Knowing how to use modifying nouns correctly increases your vocabulary and helps you sound more natural.

When a noun acts like an adjective, it cannot be plural.

> ✓ classroom time
> ✗ classrooms time

> ✓ family needs
> ✗ families needs

A. Change each phrase into a modifying noun.

1. experiences in life = _____ *life experiences* _____

2. experience in work = _____

3. time for relaxation = _____

4. time for work = _____

5. stress in a job = _____

6. stress in families = _____

7. vacation in the summer = _____

8. policy for vacations = _____

9. year of school = _____

10. schedule for work = _____

11. president of a company = _____

12. email from work = _____

B. Order the words. Write a question.

1. your / How long / year / is / school

   <u>How long is your school year?</u>

2. do you / vacation / How many / get / days of

   _____?

3. your / What / vacation / do you / on / summer / do

   _____?

4. your / What are / vacation / this year / plans

   _____?

5. How often / from home / your / do you / check / email / work

   _____?

6. What / vacation / your / is / policy / employer's

   _____?

7. your / What time / you / do / take / break / lunch

   _____?

8. favorite / your / is / spot / What / vacation

   _____?

C. Compare your answers for Activity B with a partner. Then take turns asking and answering the questions.

 D. Go online for more practice with modifying nouns.

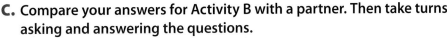

WRITING

 **UNIT OBJECTIVE** ▶▶▶▶ At the end of this unit, you will write a paragraph about how much vacation you need. Your paragraph will include specific information from the readings and your own ideas.

| Writing Skill | Using correct paragraph structure |

A **paragraph** is a group of sentences about one main idea. Paragraphs for school and university work usually have the following parts.

- **A topic sentence:** This sentence tells the main idea of the whole paragraph. It is usually the first or second sentence in the paragraph.
- **Supporting sentences:** These sentences explain the main idea. They often give examples and details.
- **A concluding sentence:** This sentence ends the paragraph. Sometimes it tells the reader the main idea again. Some paragraphs, especially short ones, do not have a concluding sentence.

A strong paragraph is important for good writing.

Note: At the beginning of a paragraph, the writer indents the first line. This means the line starts after five letter spaces.

A. WRITING MODEL Read the model paragraphs. Underline the topic sentence, the three supporting sentences, and the concluding sentence. Then write *TS* (topic sentence), *SS* (supporting sentence), or *CS* (concluding sentence) above each sentence.

1. *TS*
   <u>Vacations are not the right answer to worker stress.</u> First of all, one or two vacations a year cannot reduce the stress of many days of long work hours. Also, vacations can actually be very stressful because they are expensive. Finally, people lived for thousands of years without vacations. Vacations are not necessary.

2. In many countries, workers don't have much vacation time, but in some countries in Europe, long summer vacations are the law. In Sweden and Finland employers must give employees a four-week-long summer vacation. In Norway and Denmark employees have 15 to 18 days

off at a time in the summer. In Greece all workers get two complete weeks off in the summer. In Europe, long summer vacations are part of the work calendar.

3.   Long vacations are good for my health, my family, and my work. I can really relax and sleep better because I'm not thinking about schedules and work. Also my family connects better because we are not busy and worried about what is next. Finally, I come back to work with better and more creative ideas. For these reasons, I take long vacations with my family every summer.

B. Read the sentences in each group. Put the sentences into the order of a paragraph. Number them 1–5.

1. Chinese Golden Week

_____ Finally, with the Golden Week policy, a worker is sure to have a vacation with pay every year.

_____ First of all, many Chinese people work far away from their hometowns, and Golden Week gives them enough time to travel back home.

_____ For these three reasons, the Golden Week policy is a good idea.

_____ Many people in China like the Golden Week vacation policy because it improves workers' lives in the following ways.

_____ Also, the Golden Week policy makes it easy to plan a big family celebration because everyone has a vacation at the same time.

Chinese families spend time together during Golden Week.

2. **The Truth about Summer Vacations**

____ Long summer vacations are not learning opportunities.

____ Children just watch TV and play video games for months in the summer.

____ First of all, most parents work, so children are alone at home.

____ For these reasons, most children do not learn new skills in the summer.

____ Because it is dangerous to go outside without an adult, children stay inside their homes.

3. **Summer Learning Opportunities**

____ First of all, children can discover nature by hiking in the mountains or going to beaches.

____ Finally, as they get older, teenagers can get work experience in the summer.

____ Summer vacation is an opportunity to learn about the world.

____ All these experiences are possible on long summer vacations.

____ Also, they can travel abroad to learn new languages.

C. Write the sentences from one of the topics in B in the form of a paragraph.

_____

_____

_____

_____

_____

_____

iQ ONLINE **D. Go online for more practice using correct paragraph structure.**

You can combine two sentences with *because*. *Because* introduces the reason for a situation or state.

> Bob is a doctor. (reason)　→　He cannot take long vacations. (situation)
> Bob cannot take long vacations **because** he is a doctor.
> **Because** Bob is a doctor, he cannot take long vacations.

> I worked many hours yesterday. (reason)　→　I am tired. (state)
> I am tired **because** I worked many hours yesterday.
> **Because** I worked many hours yesterday, I am tired.

- There is no comma when *because* is in the middle of the sentence. There is a comma when the sentence begins with *because*.

- When the subject in both parts of the sentence is the same, use a pronoun in the second part of the sentence.

> ✓ **Lucy** is tired because **she** worked many hours yesterday.
> ✗ **Lucy** is tired because **Lucy** worked many hours yesterday.

A. Write two sentences with *because*. Remember that *because* introduces the reason.

1. People need a break from work.　→　People take vacations.

   a. *People take vacations because they need a break from work.*

   b. *Because people need a break from work, they take vacations.*

2. Truck drivers work long hours.　→　Truck drivers have a lot of job stress.

   a. _____

   b. _____

3. Some employees don't have paid vacation.　→　Some employees don't take vacations.

   a. _____

   _____

   b. _____

   _____

4. Some employees have family needs. → Some employees have special schedules.

a. _____

_____

b. _____

_____

5. Children worked on farms. → Children had long summer vacations.

a. _____

_____

b. _____

_____

B. Complete each sentence with your own idea. Read your sentences to a partner.

1. I like to go on vacation in the summer because _____

_____.

2. Today, people have a lot of work stress because _____

_____.

C. Go online for more practice combining sentences with *because*.

D. Go online for the grammar expansion.

Vacations give families time to spend together.

 **UNIT OBJECTIVE** ▶▶▶▶ In this assignment, you are going to write a paragraph to answer the question, "How much vacation do you need?" As you prepare your paragraph, think about the Unit Question, "Why is vacation important?" Use information from Reading 1, Reading 2, the unit video, and your work in this unit to support your paragraph. Refer to the Self-Assessment checklist on page 70.

 Go to the Online Writing Tutor for a writing model and alternate Unit Assignments.

PLAN AND WRITE

A. BRAINSTORM Complete the activities.

1. Discuss the question with a partner. How many vacation days do you need in a year? Why do you need that number of vacation days?

2. Write four reasons you need vacation time.

   I need to spend time with my family.

3. Choose the three best reasons. You will use them in Activity B.

Tip for Success

The commas in the sentences in Activity B all come after an introductory word or phrase (*First of all, Finally, For these three reasons*). Remember to use commas after introductory phrases.

B. PLAN Write your ideas. Complete the sentences.

Topic sentence: I need _____ vacation days each year.

   Reason 1: First of all, I need _____ vacation days because _____

   _____.

   Reason 2: I also need them because _____

   _____.

   Reason 3: Finally, I really need that many days because _____

   _____.

Concluding sentence: For these three reasons, I need at least _____ vacation days.

C. **WRITE** Use your **PLAN** notes to write your paragraph. Go to *iQ Online* to use the Online Writing Tutor.

1. Write your paragraph. Remember to indent the first line.

2. Look at the Self-Assessment checklist to guide your writing.

REVISE AND EDIT

A. **PEER REVIEW** Read your partner's paragraph. Then go online and use the Peer Review worksheet. Discuss the review with your partner.

B. **REWRITE** Based on your partner's review, revise and rewrite your paragraph.

C. **EDIT** Complete the Self-Assessment checklist as you prepare to write the final draft of your paragraph. Be prepared to hand in your work or discuss it in class.

Yes	No	SELF-ASSESSMENT
☐	☐	Does your topic sentence give the main idea of your paragraph?
☐	☐	Do your supporting sentences give examples and details to support your main idea?
☐	☐	Does your paragraph have a concluding sentence?
☐	☐	Do you use the word *because* correctly to give reasons?
☐	☐	Is the first line of your paragraph indented?
☐	☐	Does every sentence begin with a capital letter and end with final punctuation?
☐	☐	Does the paragraph include vocabulary from the unit?
☐	☐	Did you check a dictionary for correct spelling?

D. **REFLECT** Go to the Online Discussion Board to discuss these questions.

1. What is something new you learned in this unit?

2. Look back at the Unit Question—Why is vacation important? Is your answer different now than when you started the unit? If yes, how is it different? Why?

TRACK YOUR SUCCESS

Circle the words you have learned in this unit.

Nouns	Verbs	Adjectives
attitude 🔑 AWL	compete	abroad 🔑
average 🔑	connect 🔑	likely 🔑
benefit 🔑 AWL	discover 🔑	positive 🔑 AWL
employee	improve 🔑	
policy AWL	produce 🔑	
	reduce 🔑	
	rest 🔑	

🔑 Oxford 2000 keywords

AWL Academic Word List

Check (✓) the skills you learned. If you need more work on a skill, refer to the page(s) in parentheses.

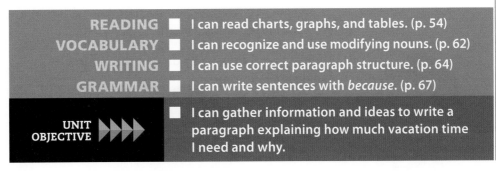

READING ☐ I can read charts, graphs, and tables. (p. 54)

VOCABULARY ☐ I can recognize and use modifying nouns. (p. 62)

WRITING ☐ I can use correct paragraph structure. (p. 64)

GRAMMAR ☐ I can write sentences with *because*. (p. 67)

UNIT OBJECTIVE ▶▶▶▶ ☐ I can gather information and ideas to write a paragraph explaining how much vacation time I need and why.

UNIT

4

Physiology

READING ▶ identifying the topic sentence in a paragraph
VOCABULARY ▶ parts of speech
WRITING ▶ writing a topic sentence
GRAMMAR ▶ sentences with *when*

UNIT QUESTION

What makes you laugh?

A Discuss these questions with your classmates.

1. When was the last time you laughed? Why did you laugh?

2. Why is it important to laugh?

3. Look at the photos. Why do you think these people are laughing?

UNIT
OBJECTIVE ▶▶▶▶ Read the articles. Gather information and ideas to write
a paragraph about what makes you or someone you
know laugh.

B Listen to *The Q Classroom* online.
Then match the ideas in the box to
the students below.

a. funny TV shows	b. comedians	c. family
d. silly things	e. unexpected things	

What makes them laugh?	
Sophy	a. funny TV shows
Yuna	
Felix	
Marcus	b. comedians

C Go to the Online Discussion Board to discuss the Unit Question
with your classmates.

D Look at the photos below. What is happening in each photo? Why is each person laughing? Write your idea for each photo. Then discuss your ideas in a group.

1. _____

2. _____

3. _____

4. _____

E Discuss these questions in a group.

1. Do you laugh for the same reasons as the people in the pictures?

2. Tell the group about a time you laughed a lot. Why did you laugh?

READING

UNIT OBJECTIVE ▶▶▶▶

You are going to read an online article about the different reasons people laugh. Use the article to gather information and ideas for your Unit Assignment.

PREVIEW THE READING

Tip for Success

Many adjectives have the same form as verbs in the simple past, for example, *surprised* and *embarrassed*.

A. VOCABULARY Here are some words from Reading 1. Read the sentences. Then write each underlined word next to the correct definition.

1. I think laughter is <u>natural</u>, just like eating and sleeping.

2. I don't really like parties, but I <u>pretend</u> to have fun.

3. I know it is true because Mary told me. She is an <u>honest</u> person.

4. I always feel <u>nervous</u> when my brother drives. He's not a good driver.

5. I don't like to speak in front of the class. I feel <u>embarrassed</u>.

6. The news didn't <u>surprise</u> Jim. Someone told him about it earlier.

7. Wear sunglasses to <u>protect</u> your eyes from the sun.

a. _____ (*verb*) to keep someone or something safe

b. _____ (*verb*) to try to make someone believe something that is not true

c. _____ (*verb*) to do something that someone does not expect

d. _____ (*adjective*) not made or caused by people

e. _____ (*adjective*) shy or worried about what other people think of you

f. _____ (*adjective*) saying what is true

g. _____ (*adjective*) worried or afraid about what may happen

B. Go online for more practice with the vocabulary.

C. PREVIEW Read the article's headings. What three questions does the article ask about laughter?

Question 1: _____

Question 2: _____

Question 3: _____

_____

D. QUICK WRITE Read the questions from the article's headings again. What do you think? Write a response to each question before you read the article. Remember to use this section for your Unit Assignment.

WORK WITH THE READING

A. Read the magazine article and gather information about what makes people laugh.

What Is Laughter?

1   Laughter is **natural** for people. We start to laugh at about four months of age. We start to laugh even before we start to speak!

2   Laughter connects us with other people. We laugh more when we are with other people. Studies find that we are 30 times more likely to laugh with other people than alone. Laughter is also contagious[1]. When one person laughs, other people begin to laugh, too.

3   It is difficult to **pretend** to laugh. Laughter is **honest**. Try to laugh right now. It's difficult, isn't it? When people pretend to laugh, most people know it's not real. Studies show that people don't like the sound of fake[2] laughter.

When do people laugh?

4   Only 10 to 20 percent of laughter is about something funny. Most laughter is about being friendly with other people. Most laughter says, "I don't want to compete with you. I want to be friendly with you." This kind of laughter brings people together.

5   We often laugh when we feel **nervous**. At the beginning of meetings someone often tells a joke when everyone feels nervous. It is usually a small joke, but we laugh a lot. Our laughter helps us relax.

6   Sometimes we laugh because we think we are better than other people. When we laugh at another

---

[1] **contagious:** passing from one person to another person very quickly
[2] **fake:** not real

person, we are saying, "I am better than you." This kind of laughter makes others feel bad. Sometimes we laugh because we feel **embarrassed**.

What is funny?

7   Some things are funny because we don't expect them. When a joke begins, we already have an idea about the end. We think we know the end, but then the joke ends in a different way. The end of the joke **surprises** us. It makes us laugh.

8   Silly³ things are sometimes funny. We laugh at jokes about people and their mistakes because we know something they don't know. We think we are better than they are.

Why doesn't everyone laugh at the same joke?

9   Not everyone has the same sense of humor⁴. Some people think a joke is funny, but other people don't think so. People have different ideas about what is funny.

10   Our idea of what is funny changes with time. For young children, the world is new. Many things surprise them, so they laugh a lot. Teenagers often worry about what others think of them. They laugh to **protect** themselves. Adults laugh at themselves and other people with similar problems. They laugh at things that give them stress. Our reasons for laughter change over time.

Laughter is natural for people.

³ **silly:** not serious; stupid

⁴ **sense of humor:** ability to feel or understand what is funny

---

B. Circle the best answer according to Reading 1.

1. Why do we laugh?
   a. because our parents teach us to laugh
   b. because it is a natural thing to do

2. When do people laugh most often?
   a. when they are alone
   b. when they are with other people

3. What is funny?
   a. something we know very well
   b. something surprising or silly

4. Why doesn't everyone laugh at the same joke?
   a. Different things make different people laugh.
   b. Most people don't laugh in front of others.

C. Read the statements. Write *T* (true) or *F* (false). Then correct the false statements. In what paragraph is the information found?

__T__ 1. People sometimes laugh when they are surprised. __7__

_____

____ 2. People like it when others pretend to laugh. ____

_____

____ 3. Young children often laugh because the world surprises them. ____

_____

____ 4. A small joke at the beginning of a meeting makes us relax. ____

_____

D. Complete the sentences with the correct word from the box.

contagious	friendly	social
embarrassed	honest	

1. Most people laugh as a way to show they are _____ .

2. We laugh more when we are with other people because laughter is

_____ .

3. If I am laughing, you are likely to start laughing because laughter is

_____ .

4. People do not like the sound of fake laughter because laughter is

_____ .

5. Some people laugh when they feel nervous or _____ .

E. Write the number of the paragraph where each reason for laughter appears. Then write information from the article that supports each reason.

1. __2__ We laugh to connect with others.

   Support: _____ *We laugh more when we are with other people.* _____

2. ___ We laugh to show we are friendly.

   Support: _____

3. ___ We laugh to protect ourselves from others.

   Support: _____

4. ___ We laugh because someone tells a funny joke.

   Support: _____

5. ___ We laugh at our own problems.

   Support: _____

WRITE WHAT YOU THINK

A. Ask and answer the questions with a partner. Check (✓) "never," "sometimes," or "often." Add one more question to the chart.

Do you laugh . . .	Never	Sometimes	Often
1. . . . when you are nervous?	☐	☐	☐
2. . . . when you hear a joke?	☐	☐	☐
3. . . . when you hear other people laugh?	☐	☐	☐
4. . . . when you are embarrassed?	☐	☐	☐
5. . . . when something surprises you?	☐	☐	☐
6. . . . when _____ ?	☐	☐	☐

B. Choose one of the questions and write a response in a complete sentence. Look back at your Quick Write on page 76 as you think about what you learned.

Question: ___

My response: _____

_____

_____

_____

The **topic sentence** explains the main idea of a paragraph. Other sentences in a paragraph support the topic sentence. Often, the topic sentence is the first sentence of a paragraph, but sometimes it is the second sentence or the last sentence. Finding the topic sentence helps you quickly understand what the paragraph is about.

> **Laughter is natural.** We start to laugh at about four months of age. We start to laugh even before we start to speak!
>
> **Laughter is social.** We laugh more when we are with other people. Studies find that we are 30 times more likely to laugh with other people than alone. Laughter is also contagious. When one person laughs, other people begin to laugh, too. People connect to each other with laughter.
>
> It is difficult to pretend to laugh. **Laughter is honest.** Try to laugh right now. It's difficult, isn't it? When people pretend to laugh, most people know it's not real. Studies show that people don't like the sound of fake laughter.

A. Go back to Reading 1 on pages 76–77. Circle the topic sentence in each paragraph and write *TS* next to it.

B. Read the paragraphs below. Circle the topic sentence in each paragraph and write *TS* next to it.

1.   Robert Provine studied people and laughter. He discovered that people laugh when they want to be friendly. He watched people in the city walking and shopping. He found that 80 to 90 percent of laughter came after sentences like "I know" or "I'll see you later." People didn't laugh because someone said something funny. People laughed because they wanted to be friendly with each other.

2.   Laughter happens at certain times in a conversation. People laugh more when they speak than when they listen. Pay attention to conversations around you. You will discover that the speaker in a conversation laughs more often. Also, laughter almost always comes at the end of a sentence or a thought. For example, a person might say, "He went to the wrong store! Ha! Ha! Ha!" The person does not say, "He went—Ha! Ha! Ha!—to the wrong store!"

 C. Go online for more practice identifying the topic sentence.

READING 2 | Laugh More and Stress Less

UNIT OBJECTIVE ▶▶▶▶

You are going to read an online article about laughter's effect on the brain. Use the article to gather information and ideas for your Unit Assignment.

PREVIEW THE READING

Vocabulary Skill Review

In Unit 3, you learned about modifying nouns. Look at sentence 7 in Activity A. Circle the modifying noun.

A. **VOCABULARY** Here are some words from Reading 2. Read the sentences. Then write each underlined word next to the correct definition.

1. <u>Breathe</u> deeply. It helps you relax.

2. I read at a slow <u>rate</u>. I read only a few words per minute.

3. She needs quiet to <u>concentrate</u> on her homework.

4. Laughter has a good <u>effect</u> on your body and your health.

5. Eating healthy food and getting exercise can <u>prevent</u> many illnesses.

6. I want more laughter in my life. I want to <u>increase</u> how much I laugh.

7. Turn your phone off so you are not <u>distracted</u> during class time.

a. _____ (*verb*) to take in and let out air through your nose and mouth

b. _____ (*verb*) to cause the amount, level, or number of something to go up

c. _____ (*verb*) to give all your attention to something

d. _____ (*verb*) to stop someone from doing something; to stop something from happening

e. _____ (*noun*) a change that happens because of something

f. _____ (*noun*) the speed of something or how often something happens

g. _____ (*adjective*) not paying attention to something because you are thinking about something else

 B. Go online for more practice with the vocabulary.

When you skim a text, remember to read the title, headings, and first and last sentence of each paragraph.

C. PREVIEW Skim the article and then read the question below. Circle *Yes* or *No*.

Does laughing make you a better student?　　　Yes　　　No

D. QUICK WRITE Think about the last time you laughed out loud. Write a few sentences about how you felt. Remember to use this section for your Unit Assignment.

WORK WITH THE READING

A. Read the article and gather information about what makes you laugh.

Laugh More and Stress Less

Meet Martin

1　Martin is a university student. He is studying for a big exam. He has been studying many hours. He is worried about the exam. Martin cannot **concentrate**. He is looking at his book, but he is thinking about other things. He is **distracted**. He can't remember the information he has studied. What can Martin do to get ready for the exam? He can go out with a friend and laugh a little. Seriously! Laughter quickly reduces the **effects** of stress on your brain.

Stress and Your Body

2　Stress has many effects on your body and brain. Your brain needs oxygen[1] to think. Stress reduces oxygen in your body. When you laugh, you **breathe** deeply. When you laugh, your heart **rate** goes up. More oxygen goes to your brain. The oxygen helps you think better.

Concentration

3　Stress reduces your ability to concentrate. When you feel stress, your brain thinks something bad will happen. Your brain is looking around for possible problems. Your brain is looking for danger. You are distracted, and you cannot concentrate.

[1] oxygen: air

4   Laughter immediately reduces stress. Laughter sends a message to your brain. "I'm OK. I'm safe." Then your brain stops looking for danger. After you laugh, your brain relaxes, and you can concentrate on your studies.

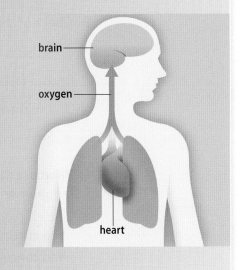

Memory

5   Stress reduces your memory and ability to learn. Stress reduces your ability to concentrate. Without concentration, you cannot learn new information. With stress, you can forget things you learned before. Stress makes it harder for your brain to find information. Laughter helps you relax, and when you relax, you can remember the information you learned.

Feelings

6   Studying for a test can make you feel lonely. You may worry you are not learning as fast as others. Laughter is a fast way to connect with other people. When you laugh with others, you feel close to them. Laughter breaks your feeling of loneliness and worry. It makes you feel stronger.

7   When you have too much stress from your studies, you can feel angry or sad. When you laugh, you let go of the bad feelings. You forget your anger and sadness. You immediately feel a little bit better.

Laughter Lasts

8   The more often you laugh, the better. When you laugh often, stress has less effect on you and your brain. Laughter **prevents** stress.

9   So next time you have a big test, take some time to find what's funny in life! It's good for you, and it **increases** your brain power!

B. Check (✓) the main idea of the article.

☐ 1. Stress is bad for your health.

☐ 2. You feel less stress when you laugh often.

☐ 3. Laughter helps you do well in your studies.

☐ 4. Stress helps you concentrate.

C. What are the effects of stress on the body? What are the effects of laughter on the body? Write the sentences in the correct column.

You are distracted.	You forget what you studied.
You concentrate.	You have less oxygen in the brain.
You feel angry or sad.	You increase oxygen in the brain.
You feel close to others.	You relax.
You feel lonely.	You remember information.

Effects of Stress	Effects of Laughter

D. Match the beginning of each sentence with the correct ending.

1. When you breathe deeply, ____ a. you expect bad things to happen.

2. When you cannot concentrate, ____ b. you do not learn new information.

3. When you laugh often, ____ c. you feel safe and OK.

4. When you feel stress, ____ d. stress has less effect on your brain.

5. When you laugh, ____ e. oxygen goes to the brain.

E. The article says you should stop and have a good laugh before you take a test. Why? Write three reasons from the article.

F. Look back at your Quick Write on page 82. Revise and add information to your answers based on what you learned from the reading.

 G. Go online to read *My Funny Friend* and check your comprehension.

 # WRITE WHAT YOU THINK

A. Discuss the questions in a group. Look back at your Quick Write on page 82 as you think about what you learned.

1. Martin feels stress from his studies. Do you feel stress from your studies? What happens to you when you feel stress?

2. What do you do to reduce stress?

3. Can laughter be a way to reduce the stress you feel? Why? Why not?

 B. Go online to watch the video about laughter clubs. Then check your comprehension.

Writing **Tip**

Remember to use specific details, such as examples and explanations, to support your topic sentence.

C. Think about the unit video, Reading 1, and Reading 2 as you discuss the questions. Then choose one question and write a response.

1. Do you want to laugh more? Why? Why not?

2. How can laughter improve our lives?

Question: ____

My response: _____

_____

_____

Vocabulary Skill Parts of speech

When you see a word you don't know in a text, it helps to **identify the part of speech** of the word. Nouns, verbs, adjectives, and adverbs are examples of parts of speech. Knowing the part of speech helps you better understand the meaning and use of the word. If you aren't sure, you can find the part of speech for the vocabulary words in this book on the last page of each unit (in *Track Your Success*). You can also find the part of speech in a dictionary.

> noun *(n.)* a person, place, object, or idea *He tells funny **jokes** at **dinner**.*
> verb *(v.)* an action *He **tells** funny jokes at dinner.*
> adjective *(adj.)* describes a noun *He tells **funny** jokes at dinner.*
> adverb *(adv.)* describes an action *We all laugh **loudly** at his jokes.*

When you know the part of speech, you can use the word correctly in a sentence.

> Correct: *She laughs at my jokes.*
> Incorrect: *She laughter at my jokes.*

 **Tip for Success**

Write new vocabulary in a list. Include the part of speech and a definition for each word. Review the vocabulary list every day.

A. Read each sentence in the chart below. Write the part of speech of the underlined word. Then check your answers in a dictionary.

	Part of Speech
1. I feel <u>embarrassed</u> when I meet new people.	
2. Laughter stops <u>anger</u>.	
3. Laughter <u>protects</u> you from some illnesses.	
4. We <u>breathe</u> differently when we laugh.	
5. Laughter has many healthy <u>effects</u> on the body.	
6. I <u>laugh</u> a lot with my friends.	
7. The <u>whole</u> group laughs together in a laughing exercise.	
8. Laughter makes you breathe <u>quickly</u>.	

B. The underlined words are the incorrect part of speech. Rewrite each word using the correct part of speech. Use a dictionary to help you.

1. They are laughing because they are <u>embarrassment</u>. _____

2. I want to <u>introduction</u> you to my friend John. _____

3. Laughter is a gift from <u>natural</u>. _____

4. Try to <u>breath</u> deeply. _____

5. Laughter exercises can <u>prevention</u> some illnesses. _____

6. Her <u>angry</u> goes away when she laughs. _____

iQ ONLINE   **C.** Go online for more practice with parts of speech.

WRITING

UNIT OBJECTIVE ▶▶▶▶ At the end of this unit, you will write a paragraph about what makes you laugh. Your paragraph will include specific information from the readings and your own ideas.

Writing Skill · Writing a topic sentence

The topic sentence introduces the main idea of the paragraph. It tells what the paragraph is about.

> **There are different kinds of laughter.** Some laughter is short and light. It comes from the throat. Other laughter comes from the stomach. This laughter is deep and loud. In addition, each person's laughter is different. No two laughs are exactly the same.

Writing a good topic sentence will make your writing clearer to readers.

A. Go back to Reading 2 on pages 82 and 83. Underline the topic sentences of paragraphs 2–8. Write TS next to the sentence.

B. **WRITING MODEL** Match each model topic sentence with the correct paragraph. Write the topic sentence on the line.

> ~~When Bob is nervous, he laughs.~~
> Mark relaxes when he laughs.
> Paula laughs when she hears something funny.
> Sam laughs to be friendly.
> When Jenny is with people, she laughs.

1. _When Bob is nervous, he laughs._

   For example, he laughs when he gets in trouble. He also laughs when he speaks in front of the class. In new situations, he makes jokes. Generally, my friend laughs when he is nervous.

2. _____

   For example, he laughs when he meets new people. He also laughs when he is with good friends. He always laughs. It's clear that he laughs to make people feel good.

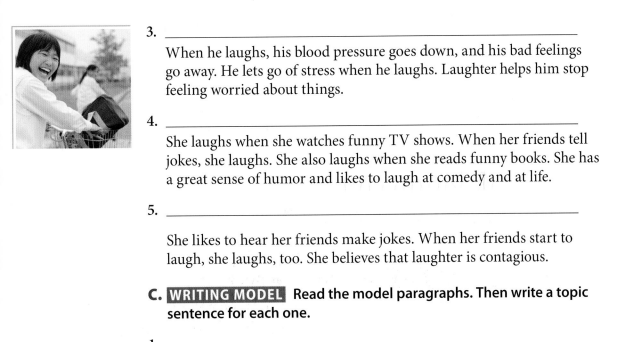

3. _____

When he laughs, his blood pressure goes down, and his bad feelings go away. He lets go of stress when he laughs. Laughter helps him stop feeling worried about things.

4. _____

She laughs when she watches funny TV shows. When her friends tell jokes, she laughs. She also laughs when she reads funny books. She has a great sense of humor and likes to laugh at comedy and at life.

5. _____

She likes to hear her friends make jokes. When her friends start to laugh, she laughs, too. She believes that laughter is contagious.

C. **WRITING MODEL** Read the model paragraphs. Then write a topic sentence for each one.

1. _____

She goes there once a month and does laughing exercises in her group. After she practices laughing for two hours, She feels great. Lea laughs a lot at the laughing club.

2. _____

Laughter makes you breathe quickly. It increases your heart rate. It turns your face red. Ten to fifteen minutes of laughing burns 50 calories! Laughter exercises your whole body.

3. _____

Feelings like fear, anger, and frustration can cause stress. These bad feelings can bring you down. Laughter helps you let go of bad feelings.

4. _There is **one important action** that everyone does ~~doing~~ in laughter exercise._

In one laughter exercise, we stand in a circle. We put our hands on our face or stomach. Then we make "ha ha" or "hee hee" sounds. Everyone in the circle starts laughing. That is how we practice laughing in our club.

5. _There are many benefits of laughing which makes people to go **to the** laughing **club**_

Some people go to laughter clubs to learn how to laugh more so they feel less pain. Some people have health problems that cause a lot of pain. Laughter reduces the pain that a person feels.

D. Read these paragraphs from the reading "The World in a City," from Unit 2. Circle each topic sentence.

1. Do you plan to visit London? There are many English sights to see, but there are many international sights, sounds, and foods too. London is a city with many different groups of people. In a visit to London, you see the world.

2. There is food from more than 55 different countries in London's restaurants. There is even food from countries such as Tanzania, Peru, and Mongolia. At food markets, you can buy vegetables and fruits from all over the world.

3. London has many festivals with food, music, art, and dance from different countries. In winter, you can celebrate Chinese New Year. In early spring, you can celebrate the Russian end of winter. In the summer, you can go to the largest Caribbean festival in the world. In the fall, you can enjoy the Indian festival of lights.

iQ ONLINE   **E.** Go online for more practice with writing a topic sentence.

You can combine two sentences with *when*.

- There is a comma if the sentence begins with *when*. There is no comma if *when* is in the middle of the sentence.
- When the subject in both sentences is the same, use a pronoun in the second part of the sentence.

They are nervous. → They laugh.	Bob laughs. → He feels less stress.
When they are nervous, they laugh.	**When** Bob laughs, he feels less stress.
They laugh **when** they are nervous.	Bob feels less stress **when** he laughs.

A. Write two sentences with *when*.

1. I go out with my friends.   →   I laugh a lot.

   a. <u>When I go out with my friends, I laugh a lot.</u>

   b. <u>I laugh a lot when I go out with my friends.</u>

2. You laugh.   →   Your heart rate increases.

   a. <u>When your heart rate increases, you laugh</u>

   b. <u>You laugh when your heart rate increase</u>

3. He sees something funny.   →   He laughs.

   a. <u>When He sees something f</u>

   b. _____

4. You laugh.   →   You use calories.

   a. _____

   b. _____

5. We hear a good joke.   →   We laugh.

   a. _____

   b. _____

6. She is nervous.   →   She laughs.

a. _____

b. _____

B. Go back to the sentences in Activity E on pages 78 and 79. Combine the sentences with *when*. For example: *When we are with other people, we laugh. We laugh when we are with other people.*

C. Complete each sentence with your own idea. Then read your sentences to a partner.

1. I laugh a lot when _____.

2. I never laugh when _____.

3. When I see someone fall, _____.

4. When I am in class, _____.

5. When I am nervous, _____.

6. When I laugh, _____.

7. When I am with my family, _____.

D. Go online for more practice with sentences with *when*.

E. Go online for the grammar expansion.

Unit Assignment | Write a paragraph about what makes people laugh

In this assignment, you are going to write a paragraph about what makes you or someone you know laugh. As you prepare your paragraph, think about the Unit Question, "What makes you laugh?" Use information from Reading 1, Reading 2, the unit video, and your work in this unit to support your paragraph. Refer to the Self-Assessment checklist on page 94.

Go to the Online Writing Tutor for a writing model and alternate Unit Assignments.

PLAN AND WRITE

A. **BRAINSTORM** Think of what makes you laugh. Look at the questions below and answer them in the chart. Then ask a partner the same questions, and complete the chart with your partner's answers.

	Who are you with when you laugh?	Where are you when you laugh?	What are you doing when you laugh?
You			
Your Partner			

> **Critical Thinking** Tip
>
> Step 2 asks you to **outline** your paragraph. **Outlining** helps you to see the different parts of your writing. It is a very good way to organize your ideas.

B. **PLAN** Follow these steps to plan your paragraph.

1. Write a topic sentence for your paragraph. For example:

   I laugh when something makes me nervous.

   I laugh when I watch funny videos on my computer.

   I laugh more when I am with my friends.

   Your topic sentence: _____.

2. Go online to complete the outline for your paragraph.

C. **WRITE** Use your **PLAN** notes to write your paragraph. Go to *iQ Online* to use the Online Writing Tutor.

1. Make sure the topic sentence introduces the main idea of the paragraph.

2. Look at the Self-Assessment checklist to guide your writing.

REVISE AND EDIT

A. **PEER REVIEW** Read your partner's paragraph. Then go online and use the Peer Review worksheet. Discuss the review with your partner.

B. **REWRITE** Based on your partner's review, revise and rewrite your paragraph.

C. **EDIT** Complete the Self-Assessment checklist as you prepare to write the final draft of your paragraph. Be prepared to hand in your work or discuss it in class.

SELF-ASSESSMENT		
Yes	**No**	
☐	☐	Does your topic sentence present your main idea clearly?
☐	☐	Do all your sentences support your topic sentence?
☐	☐	Do you use *when* to explain what makes people laugh?
☐	☐	Did you use the correct part of speech for each noun, verb, adjective, and adverb in your paragraph?
☐	☐	Does your paragraph include vocabulary from this unit?
☐	☐	Did you use a comma in sentences beginning with *When*?
☐	☐	Is your spelling correct? Check a dictionary if you are not sure.
☐	☐	Is the first line of the paragraph indented?
☐	☐	Does every sentence begin with a capital letter and end with final punctuation?

D. **REFLECT** Go to the Online Discussion Board to discuss these questions.

1. What is something new you learned in this unit?

2. Look back at the Unit Question—What makes you laugh? Is your answer different now than when you started the unit? If yes, how is it different? Why?

TRACK YOUR SUCCESS

Circle the words you have learned in this unit.

Nouns	**Verbs**	**Adjectives**
effect 🔑	breathe 🔑	distracted
rate 🔑	concentrate 🔑 AWL	embarrassed 🔑
	increase 🔑	honest 🔑
	pretend 🔑	natural 🔑
	prevent 🔑	nervous 🔑
	protect 🔑	
	surprise 🔑	

🔑 Oxford 2000 keywords

AWL Academic Word List

Check (✓) the skills you learned. If you need more work on a skill, refer to the page(s) in parentheses.

READING ☐	I can identify the topic sentence in a paragraph. (p. 80)
VOCABULARY ☐	I can identify parts of speech. (p. 86)
WRITING ☐	I can write a topic sentence. (p. 88)
GRAMMAR ☐	I can use sentences with *when*. (p. 91)
UNIT OBJECTIVE ▶▶▶ ☐	I can gather information and ideas to write a paragraph that explains what makes me or someone I know laugh.

READING ▶ identifying supporting sentences and details
VOCABULARY ▶ the prefix *un-*
WRITING ▶ writing supporting sentences and details
GRAMMAR ▶ prepositions of location

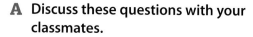

Q? UNIT QUESTION

How do sports make you feel?

A Discuss these questions with your classmates.

1. What sports do you like to play?

2. What sports do you like to watch?

3. Look at the photo. How do you think these people feel? Why?

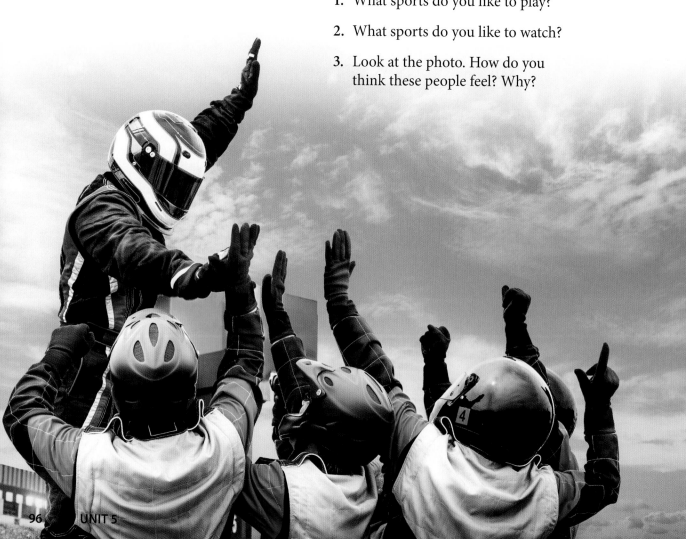

B Listen to *The Q Classroom* online. Then answer these questions.

1. Who plays sports?

2. Who watches sports?

3. Who does both?

 C Watch the video about running. Then check your comprehension.

pain *(n.)* the feeling when something hurts

muscles *(n.)* the parts of your body that make you move

natural high *(n.)* feeling very good without using drugs, often after exercising

VIDEO VOCABULARY

 D Go to the Online Discussion Board to discuss the Unit Question with your classmates.

E Work in a group. Write three adjectives to describe each sport.

| 1 | 2 | 3 | 4 |
| soccer* | swimming | golf | hockey |

_____ _____ _____ _____

_____ _____ _____ _____

_____ _____ _____ _____

F Check (✓) the sports that you do and the places you play. Then discuss the questions with a group.

Sports

☐ basketball   ☐ soccer   ☐ baseball
☐ swimming   ☐ golf   ☐ tennis
☐ volleyball   ☐ cricket   ☐ running

Places

☐ street   ☐ stadium   ☐ park
☐ pool   ☐ track   ☐ golf course
☐ field   ☐ beach   ☐ court
☐ gym

1. What kind of sports do people play in each place you checked? Talk about the sports above and other sports you know.

2. In which of the places can you play more than one sport?

3. Are there other places where you can play sports? Where?

---

* **soccer:** In the United States this sport is called soccer. In the rest of the world it is called football.

READING 1 | A Super Soccer Fan

UNIT OBJECTIVE ▶▶▶▶

You are going to read an article by a soccer fan from Brazil. Use the article to gather information and ideas for your Unit Assignment.

PREVIEW THE READING

Vocabulary Skill Review

In Unit 4, you learned about parts of speech. Remember to pay attention to the part of speech of each vocabulary word. This helps you to use the word correctly.

A. VOCABULARY Here are some words from Reading 1. Read the sentences. Then write each <u>underlined</u> word next to the correct definition.

1. Many people like soccer. It is a <u>popular</u> sport.

2. World Cup soccer games are <u>exciting</u>.

3. <u>According to</u> my friend, the team's new soccer player is really good.

4. Please turn down the <u>volume</u> on the TV. It's too loud.

5. I don't <u>notice</u> what color most teams wear.

6. That man looks <u>familiar</u>. I remember him from somewhere.

7. This shirt doesn't <u>fit</u>. Do you have a bigger one?

8. I am a <u>fan</u> of basketball. I watch all the games.

a. _____ (*verb*) to be the right size, shape, or type for someone or something

b. _____ (*verb*) to see or pay attention to someone or something

c. _____ (*noun*) a person who is very enthusiastic about a sport

d. _____ (*noun*) the amount of sound that something makes

e. _____ (*adjective*) causing you to have strong feelings of happiness and interest

f. _____ (*adjective*) liked by many people

g. _____ (*adjective*) that you know well

h. _____ (*preposition*) as someone or something says

iQ ONLINE **B.** Go online for more practice with the vocabulary.

C. **PREVIEW** Skim the web post. Answer the questions.

1. What is the title of the post?

2. Who is the author of the post?

3. What is the post about?

4. What is the name of the team in the photos?

D. **QUICK WRITE** What do sports fans do to show support for their favorite team? Write a list. Remember to use this section for your Unit Assignment.

WORK WITH THE READING

A. Read the article and gather information on how sports make you feel.

A Super Soccer Fan

1   I'm a huge soccer **fan**. I love my team, the Corinthians Football Club in São Paulo, Brazil. In fact, I'm crazy about them! And I'm not alone. **According to** statistics, the Corinthians are the favorite team of 15 percent of the Brazilian population. That's about 25 million people! The Corinthians are the second most **popular** team in Brazil. The most popular team, the Flamengo Football Club of Rio de Janeiro, has over 35 million fans.

2   I go to lots of Corinthians games because they're fun and **exciting**. Before the game, fans meet in the parking lot. They talk about the game and have something to eat. During the game, it's very noisy. There's lots of cheering[1] and shouting. Some people chant[2] and jump around.

3   I always dress in special clothes for the games. I wear a black and white Corinthians shirt. Sometimes I wear red, too, because that's

another Corinthians team color. When I go to important games, I wear my special hat. It's big and funny, and black and white, of course. People really **notice** me when I wear it!

4   I sometimes buy official Corinthians shirts at the team store. They're beautiful. They have large black numbers and the names of players on the back. Some customers complain that the official shirts are expensive. Some cost a hundred dollars. That's a lot of money for a shirt!

[1] **cheering:** shouting to show you like a team
[2] **chant:** to sing or shout a word or phrase many times

5   When I was a boy, I was a Corinthians fan, too. I went to lots of games with my father and my brother. We always took snacks and juice, and we had lots of fun. I have some of my old Corinthians clothes. They don't **fit** me now, but my son likes them.

6   My son sometimes goes to games with me, and we also watch games on TV. When we watch games on TV, we turn the **volume**

up really loud, and we pretend we're at the game. My wife usually turns the volume down so she can read her book.

7   Maybe you're not **familiar** with the Corinthians Football Club, but you're probably familiar with the teams in your city and country. You may not be a big soccer fan, but you probably know lots of soccer fans!

Fernando Mendes

B. Circle the answer that best completes each statement.

1. Fernando started going to Corinthian games with his _____.
   a. father   b. son   c. wife

2. Fernando takes his _____ to games now.
   a. father   b. son   c. wife

3. Fernando likes the games because they are _____.
   a. fun and exciting
   b. important and popular
   c. familiar and traditional

C. What do you know about Fernando Mendes? Where is the information in the reading? Check the statements you know to be true and write the paragraph number.

What do you know?   Where did you find the information?

☑ **1.** Fernando is a fan of the Corinthians.   _Paragraph #1_

☐ **2.** He has a brother.   _____

☐ **3.** He plays soccer.   _____

☐ **4.** He likes the noise of a soccer game.   _____

☐ **5.** He has a son.   _____

☐ **6.** He has a sister.   _____

☐ **7.** His wife doesn't like soccer.   _____

☐ **8.** His father was a Corinthians fan.   _____

☐ **9.** Fernando likes to have fun.   _____

☐ **10.** He buys Corinthian shirts at the team store.   _____

D. The following statements are not true. Change one word in each statement to make it true.

1. The Flamingo Club is less popular than the Corinthians. _____

_____

2. After the game, Corinthian fans eat together and talk about the game in the parking lot. _____

_____

3. The Corinthian colors are blue, white, and black. _____

_____

4. Fernando was a Corinthian fan when he was a baby. _____

_____

5. The official team shirts cost ten dollars. _____

_____

E. Look back at your Quick Write on page 100. What do soccer fans do? Add any new information you learned from the article.

F. Circle the answer that best completes the statement. Then answer the question.

1. People in Brazil like soccer _____ they do in my country.

    a. more than   b. less than   c. the same amount

2. List details from the article and from experiences in your country to explain your answer.

G. What do you think—why does Fernando like the Corinthians so much? How does watching soccer make him feel?

WRITE WHAT YOU THINK

A. Discuss the questions in a group.

1. Are you a big sports fan? Why or why not?

2. Why do you think people like to be fans of one team?

3. What is a popular team in your city? What do fans of this team do? What do they wear?

B. Choose one of the questions in Activity A and write a response. Look back at your Quick Write on page 100 as you think about what you learned.

Question: ____

My response: _____

_____

_____

_____

When you read a paragraph, it's important to understand how the writer supports the main idea. Good readers learn to look for the **supporting sentences** and **details**.

Supporting sentences

After you find the main idea or topic sentence in a paragraph, look for the supporting sentences. These sentences explain more about the topic sentence. The bold sentences below support the idea expressed in the topic sentence.

> I go to lots of Corinthians games because they're fun and exciting. **Before the game, fans meet in the parking lot.** They talk about the game and have something to eat. **During the game, it's very noisy.** There's lots of cheering and shouting. Some people chant and jump around.

Details

One or more details often follow a supporting sentence. The details give additional information about the supporting sentence. Each detail in the example paragraph explains what happens at the game.

> I go to lots of Corinthians games because they're fun and exciting. Before the game, fans meet in the parking lot. **They talk about the game and have something to eat.** During the game, it's very noisy. **There's lots of cheering and shouting. Some people chant and jump around.**

Tip for Success

When you read, underline the topic sentence of a paragraph and put a check (✓) next to each supporting sentence. That way you can see how the paragraph is organized.

A. Read these sentences from Paragraph 3 of Reading 1. Write the type of sentences for each.

TS = Topic Sentence

SS = Supporting Sentence

D = Detail

1. I always dress in special clothes for the games.	TS
2. I wear a black and white Corinthians shirt.	SS
3. Sometimes I wear red, too, because that's another Corinthians team color.	
4. When I go to important games, I wear my special hat.	
5. It's big and funny, and black and white, of course.	

Critical Thinking Tip

In Activities A and B, you have to **differentiate** between the topic sentence and the supporting sentences in a paragraph. **Differentiate** means to tell the difference between the two things. It can help you understand ideas better.

B. Read these sentences from Paragraphs 4 and 5 of Reading 1. Write each type of sentence in the margin. Note: The sentences are NOT in order.

TS = Topic Sentence

SS = Supporting sentence

D = Detail

Paragraph 4	
1. That's a lot of money for a shirt!	
2. They're beautiful.	
3. Some customers complain that the official shirts are expensive.	
4. I sometimes buy official Corinthians shirts at the team store.	
5. They have large black numbers and the names of players on the back.	
Paragraph 5	
6. I have some of my old Corinthians clothes.	
7. We always took snacks and juice, and we had lots of fun.	
8. When I was a boy, I was a Corinthians fan, too.	
9. They don't fit me now, but my son likes them.	
10. I went to lots of games with my father and my brother.	

 C. Go online for more practice identifying supporting sentences and details.

READING 2 | The History of Soccer

You are going to read an article about the history of soccer. Use the article to gather information and ideas for your Unit Assignment.

PREVIEW THE READING

Vocabulary Skill Review

In Unit 4, you learned about using the dictionary to identify the part of speech of a word. Look at these words from this unit and words that are related to them. Use a dictionary to find the part of speech for each related word.

association (*noun*)

associate _____

invent (*verb*)

invention _____

A. VOCABULARY Here are some words from Reading 2. Read their definitions. Then complete each sentence.

> **association** (*noun*) a group of people who join together for a special reason
> **disorganized** (*adjective*) not planned well
> **form** (*verb*) 🔑 to start a group or organization
> **history** (*noun*) 🔑 things that happened in the past
> **invent** (*verb*) 🔑 to make or think of something for the first time
> **kick** (*verb*) 🔑 to hit a ball with your feet
> **similar** (*adjective*) 🔑 the same in some ways but not all ways
> **tie** (*noun*) 🔑 when two teams have the same score in a game

1. My son and his friends want to _____ a new game, but they can't agree on the rules.

2. The score was 2–2. The game ended in a _____.

3. I am trying to _____ a volleyball team at my school. A few students are already interested in joining.

4. My friends are part of a big _____ that buys sporting equipment for poor children.

5. He's very interested in the _____ of the Olympic Games. He knows a lot about Olympic sports from many years ago.

6. In soccer, you can't use your hands. You can only _____ the ball.

7. Baseball and cricket are _____ games.

8. Our practices are usually very _____. Our coach doesn't spend much time planning them.

🔑 Oxford 2000 keywords

B. Go online for more practice with the vocabulary.

C. PREVIEW Look at the headings and captions in the article. How does the article describe soccer?

☐ creative

☐ international

☐ new

☐ natural

☐ old

☐ popular

D. QUICK WRITE What do you know about the history of soccer? Write a few sentences. Remember to use this section for your Unit Assignment.

WORK WITH THE READING

A. Read the article and gather information on how sports make you feel.

The History of Soccer

1   Without a doubt, soccer is the most popular sport in the world. Around 250 million people from more than 200 countries regularly play the game. About 3.5 billion fans watch the sport. During important international competitions, soccer has the highest television audience in the world.

Soccer is the most popular sport in the world.

A Long History

2   Soccer is not a new sport. Historians aren't sure exactly where or when the sport was **invented**. People all over the world played versions of the game long ago. For example, in China nearly 2,000 years ago, soldiers **kicked** a ball as part of their exercise. Five hundred years ago in Europe, large **disorganized** games in the street were common. Sometimes people were hurt or killed playing these games.

The First Soccer Association

3   Soccer became popular in England in the 1800's. Different schools, clubs, and groups played with different rules. In 1863, these English groups had meetings.

They organized the different games into one game with **similar** rules. Soon, they **formed** the Football **Association**.

4   Not everyone agreed with the new rules. Some groups wanted to hold the ball with their hands. These groups **formed** rugby clubs. Groups in the United States also wanted to use their hands in the sport. They formed "football" clubs. Americans who didn't want to use their hands called the game "soccer." *Soccer* is a short form of the word *association*.

An International Sport

5   From England, soccer began to grow. The first official **international** game of soccer was played between Scotland and England in 1872. The game ended in a 0–0 **tie**. By the 1880s, there were professional soccer teams in several parts of Europe. English players also introduced soccer to Africa, South America, and New Zealand.

6   Soccer soon became very popular all around the world. The international football federation, FIFA met for the first time in 1904. Seven countries came to the meeting. The first World Cup was in Uruguay in 1930. Only 13 countries played in the Uruguayan World Cup. That year, Uruguay won against Argentina, 4–2, in the final game.

7   The World Cup is now the most popular sporting event in the world. Many countries want to participate in the World Cup, but only 32 countries can compete. Over 720 million people around the world watch the final game of the World Cup.

8   Next time you're playing soccer with your friends, remember that you're part of a long **history** of a fun and exciting sport.

The first World Cup was in Uruguay South America in 1904.

B. Write TS next to the topic sentences and SS next to the supporting sentences.

Paragraph 1

____ a. About 3.5 billion fans watch the sport.

____ b. Soccer is the most popular sport in the world.

Paragraph 4

____ a. Some people wanted to play with their hands, so they formed rugby clubs.

____ b. Not everyone agreed with the new soccer rules.

Paragraph 5

_____ a. From England, soccer began to grow.

_____ b. By the 1880s, there were professional soccer teams in several parts of Europe.

Paragraph 6

_____ a. Soccer soon became very popular all around the world.

_____ b. The first World Cup was in Uruguay in 1930.

Paragraph 7

_____ a. Over 720 million people around the world watch the final game of the World Cup.

_____ b. The World Cup is now the biggest sports event in the world.

C. Read the sentences. Then number the events from 1–5.

_____ a. The first World Cup was played in Uruguay.

_____ b. Large disorganized games in the streets were common in Europe.

_____ c. Scotland and England played the first international soccer game.

_____ d. Groups in England formed the Football Association.

_____ e. The FIFA had its first meeting.

D. Answer the questions. Use complete sentences.

1. Why did the English schools and clubs form the Football Association in 1862?

_____

2. What two sports are similar to soccer?

_____

3. Why do Americans call the sport *soccer*, not *football*?

_____

4. How many countries played in the first World Cup?

_____

5. How many countries play in the World Cup now?

_____

WRITE WHAT YOU THINK

A. Discuss the questions in a group. Look back at your Quick Write on page 107 as you think about what you learned.

1. Why are rules important in sports? What happens if there are no rules?

2. What is your favorite sport? What do you know about the history of the sport?

B. Think about the unit video, Reading 1, and Reading 2 as you discuss these questions. Then choose one question and write a response.

1. What's the difference between sports and exercise?

2. Do you like playing sports with other people, or do you prefer sports that you can do alone, like running?

3. Do you belong to any sports clubs or groups? What do you do with your club?

Question: ____

My response: _____

_____

_____

_____

A **prefix** is a letter or group of letters at the beginning of a word. A prefix changes the meaning of a word. You can build your vocabulary by using prefixes. The prefix *un-* means "not." It gives an adjective the opposite meaning.

☐ familiar → **un**familiar (not familiar)

Only some adjectives can use the prefix *un-*:

✓ unlucky

✗ unfast

If you are unsure, check a dictionary before adding *un-* to an adjective.

A. Only some of these words can use *un-*. Look in the dictionary and find the words that use *un-*. Write the word with its prefix on the line. Write *not* + word for the other words.

1. bored ___not bored___

2. friendly ___unfriendly___

3. happy _____

4. important _____

5. exciting _____

6. natural _____

7. quiet _____

8. popular _____

9. similar _____

10. familiar _____

B. Write five sentences. Use adjectives from Activity A. Then read your sentences aloud to a partner.

1. _____

2. _____

3. _____

4. _____

5. _____

iQ ONLINE **C.** Go online for more practice with the prefix *un-*.

WRITING

UNIT OBJECTIVE ▶▶▶ At the end of this unit, you will write a paragraph about a favorite sport and its history. Your paragraph will include specific information from the readings and your own ideas.

| Writing Skill | Writing supporting sentences and details |

Supporting sentences explain the topic sentence in more detail. When you write an academic paper (for school), it is important to include two or three supporting sentences. It is also important to include **details**. Details give more information about each supporting sentence. Details include *examples*, *reasons*, *facts*, *dates*, and *numbers*.

[*SS* marks the beginning of **supporting sentences**. *D* marks the beginning of each **detail**.]

> *Basketball comes from the United States. SS In the winter of 1891, Dr. James Naismith invented the sport. D He was a physical education teacher in Massachusetts, MA. SS It was cold, so students could not exercise outside. D Dr. Naismith put a fruit basket high up in the gym and told students to throw a ball into the basket. His students loved the new game.*

It is good to write a list of every detail you can think of and then choose only the ones that support the paragraph topic.

A. Write *TS* at the beginning of the topic sentence. Write *SS* at the beginning of each supporting sentence. Write *D* at the beginning of each detail sentence.

1. ___ I like many different sports. ___ My favorite sport is volleyball. ___ I play it every Saturday in the park with my friends. ___ I also like swimming. ___ I swim two times a week in the school pool. ___ I also like to watch cricket. ___ I watch it on TV with my family on Sunday afternoons. ___ Of all these sports, my favorite is volleyball.

2. ____ My favorite sport is running. ____ I like to run outdoors. ____ I usually run in the park or on the school track. ____ I go running about three times a week. ____ I like running in the early morning when everything is fresh. ____ I usually like to run by myself. ____ It's a good time to think and clear my head. ____ And I love how good I feel after I run!

3. ____ I enjoy playing table tennis. ____ Table tennis is a great sport because it's easy to learn. ____ All you need is a friend to play with and a tennis table. ____ I play table tennis at a sports club in my neighborhood. ____ The club is very close to our school. ____ I meet my friends at the sports club after school three times a week. ____ We play for an hour to relax before we do our studies. ____ Table tennis is a great way to relax, move, and be with friends.

4. ____ Baseball is a great sport to play and watch. ____ It is a team sport. ____ There are nine players on each team. ____ Baseball is an outdoor sport, so baseball is played in the warm months of spring and summer. ____ The game has no time limits, so games can go for a very long time. ____ In 1981 one game lasted 8 hours and 25 minutes! ____ Many people enjoy sitting outdoors for hours to watch baseball games in the summer.

B. Read the supporting sentences (SS) and the details (D). Cross out the detail that does not belong.

1. SS: Golf started in Scotland about 800 years ago.
   D: Scottish Kings and queens played golf in the 1500s.
   D: The word golf means "stick."
   D: One king banned golf because people played it too much.

2. SS: In the 1800's the English brought golf to Japan.
   D: The first Japanese golf club was formed in 1903.
   D: In 2016 golf will be a sport in the Olympics.
   D: Today Japan has 2,400 golf courses.

3. SS: Tennis is not a team sport.
   D: Tennis is popular with both men and women.
   D: There are only two players in a singles game.
   D: There are four players in a doubles game.

4. SS: Tennis is a quiet game.
   D: Fans do not chant or cheer at games.
   D: In 2010 a game in Wimbledon was 11 hours long!
   D: Sometimes you can hear the players breathing!

C. **Read each topic sentence. Then choose the best supporting sentences from the box below. Write them on the lines. Do not write details yet.**

1. Sports are very popular today.

   Supporting sentence: _____

   Detail: _____

   Supporting sentence: _____

   Detail: _____

2. Many people don't know the history of their favorite sports.

   Supporting sentence: _____

   Detail: _____

   Supporting sentence: _____

   Detail: _____

Supporting sentences
Some sports are new.
Some people like to play sports in their free time.
Other people prefer to watch sports on TV.
Other sports have existed for a long time.

D. Choose the best detail from the box for each supporting sentence in Activity B. Write the details on the lines in Activity B.

> **Details**
>
> It's easy to play sports anywhere—in the park, on the street, or at school.
> Skateboarding, for example, only started in the 1950s.
> They can watch sports at home, at restaurants, or even on their phones.
> People have played different forms of soccer for at least 2,000 years.

 E. Go online for more practice writing supporting sentences and details.

Grammar   Prepositions of location

The prepositions *on*, *in*, and *at* are **prepositions of location**. They describe where something or someone is.

- Use *in* with large areas such as continents and countries.

  in Europe   **in** China   **in** Australia

- Use *in* with the meaning of inside.

  in a store   **in** a box   **in** a car

- Use *at* with these places.

  at work   **at** home   **at** school

- Use *at* when talking about activities at places or businesses with names.

  We went to a game **at** the new stadium.
  Let's play tennis **at** the Royal Racket Club.

- Use *on* with roads.

  on the street   **on** the highway   **on** Main Street

- Use *on* with most large forms of transportation.

  on a plane   **on** a ship   **on** a train   **on** a bus

A. Complete each sentence with the preposition *in*, *at*, or *on*.

1. Most people don't listen to live sports while they're _____ work.

2. He plays soccer with his friends at the park _____ Rose Street.

3. Many children play sports _____ school during their break time.

4. A lot of people play soccer _____ the street.

5. Jeff is taking a two-week vacation _____ Africa.

6. Coming home from work, my father listens to soccer _____ the car.

7. I watch sports on TV all the time _____ home.

8. We went to a rugby match _____ the Twickenham Rugby Stadium.

B. Complete each sentence with a place where you do or don't like to watch or listen to sporting events.

1. I like to listen to sporting events _____.

2. I like to watch sporting events _____.

3. I don't like to listen to sporting events _____.

4. I don't like to watch sporting events _____.

 C. Go online for more practice using prepositions of location.

D. Go online for the grammar expansion.

In this assignment, you are going to write a paragraph about your favorite sport and how it makes you feel. As you prepare to write, think about the Unit Question, "How do sports make you feel?" Use information from Reading 1, Reading 2, the unit video, and your work in this unit to support your paragraph. Refer to the Self-Assessment checklist on page 118.

iQ ONLINE   Go to the Online Writing Tutor for a writing model and alternate Unit Assignments.

Writing **Tip**

Introduce the topic early in your paragraph and only give information that supports the topic.

PLAN AND WRITE

A. BRAINSTORM Answer these questions.

1. Think about your favorite sport.

   What is my favorite sport? _____

   Why do I like it? _____

2. Talk about your favorite sport with a classmate. Ask and answer detailed questions, such as: When and where do you play or watch the sport? Do you have a favorite team or player? Where did you learn about the sport? How do you feel when you play or watch?

B. PLAN Write a topic sentence, supporting sentences, and details about how your favorite sport makes you feel. Use vocabulary words from the unit when you can.

Topic sentence: Sports make me feel _____.

Supporting sentence: _____.

Detail: _____.

Supporting sentence: _____.

Detail: _____.

Supporting sentence: _____.

Detail: _____.

Concluding sentence: _____.

C. **WRITE** Use your **PLAN** notes to write your paragraph. Go to *iQ Online* to use the Online Writing Tutor.

1. Write your paragraph. Remember to indent the first line.

2. Look at the Self-Assessment checklist to guide your writing.

REVISE AND EDIT

A. **PEER REVIEW** Read your partner's paragraph. Then go online and use the Peer Review worksheet. Discuss the review with your partner.

B. **REWRITE** Based on your partner's review, revise and rewrite your paragraph.

C. **EDIT** Complete the Self-Assessment checklist as you prepare to write the final draft of your paragraph. Be prepared to hand in your work or discuss it in class.

SELF-ASSESSMENT		
Yes	**No**	
☐	☐	Does the paragraph have supporting sentences to explain the topic sentence?
☐	☐	Does the paragraph have details such as examples, reasons, facts, dates, and numbers?
☐	☐	Do you use the prepositions of location *in, on,* and *at* correctly to describe where people do the sport?
☐	☐	Does the paragraph include vocabulary from the unit?
☐	☐	Does every sentence begin with a capital letter and end with final punctuation?
☐	☐	Is the spelling correct? Check a dictionary if you are unsure.

D. **REFLECT** Go to the Online Discussion Board to discuss these questions.

1. What is something new you learned in this unit?

2. Look back at the Unit Question—How do sports make you feel? Is your answer different now than when you started the unit? If yes, how is it different? Why?

TRACK YOUR SUCCESS

Circle the words you have learned in this unit.

Nouns
association
fan
history 🔑
tie 🔑
volume 🔑 AWL

Verbs
fit 🔑
form 🔑
invent 🔑
kick 🔑
notice 🔑

Adjectives
disorganized
exciting 🔑
familiar 🔑
popular 🔑
similar 🔑 AWL

Preposition
according to 🔑

🔑 Oxford 2000 keywords
AWL Academic Word List

Check (✓) the skills you learned. If you need more work on a skill, refer to the page(s) in parentheses.

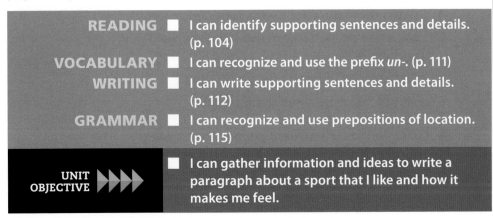

READING ☐ I can identify supporting sentences and details. (p. 104)

VOCABULARY ☐ I can recognize and use the prefix *un-*. (p. 111)

WRITING ☐ I can write supporting sentences and details. (p. 112)

GRAMMAR ☐ I can recognize and use prepositions of location. (p. 115)

UNIT OBJECTIVE ▶▶▶▶ ☐ I can gather information and ideas to write a paragraph about a sport that I like and how it makes me feel.

READING ▶ identifying pronoun referents
VOCABULARY ▶ collocations
WRITING ▶ writing concluding sentences
GRAMMAR ▶ infinitives of purpose

? UNIT QUESTION

Is it ever OK to lie?

A Discuss these questions with your classmates.

1. Look at the photo. Do you think the woman likes her gift?

2. What kinds of things do people lie about?

3. Is it ever OK to lie about those things?

B Listen to *The Q Classroom* online. Then answer the questions.

1. How did each student answer the Unit Question?

2. Sophy says that lies are fine if they don't hurt anybody. What do you think?

3. Do you agree with Felix, Marcus, Sophy, or Yuna?

 C Go to the Online Discussion Board to discuss the Unit Question with your classmates.

UNIT
OBJECTIVE ▶▶▶▶ Read the articles. Gather information and ideas to write
an opinion paragraph about the importance of honesty.

D **Complete the activities.**

1. Read each situation. Imagine you are in the situation and choose your answer. Then discuss your choice with a partner.

> **Situation 1:** A classmate asks you to go ice-skating. You don't want to. What do you say?
>
> Classmate: "Do you want to go ice-skating tomorrow?"
>
> You: "I'm sorry. I can't go. I'm busy tomorrow." **OR** "No thanks. I don't really want to go."

> **Situation 2:** Your grandmother gives you a watch. You don't like it. What do you say?
>
> Grandmother: "I got this for you."
>
> You: "Thank you. I really like it." **OR** "Thank you. It's not really my style, though."

2. Take turns role-playing each situation above with your partner. Can you think of another possible answer? You can use one of the answer choices or your own idea.

E **Read each statement in the survey. Check (✓) *Agree* or *Disagree*. Then compare your answers in a group.**

TELL *the* TRUTH!

	Agree	Disagree
1. It's possible to tell the truth all of the time.		
2. People don't want to hear the truth.		
3. A good friend always tells the truth.		
4. Some lies are OK because they make people happy.		
5. All lies are wrong.		

READING 1 | The Lies People Tell

UNIT OBJECTIVE ▶▶▶▶ You are going to read an article about the lies people tell. Use the article to gather information and ideas for your Unit Assignment.

PREVIEW THE READING

A. **VOCABULARY** Here are some words from Reading 1. Read their definitions. Then complete each sentence.

> **admit** (*verb*) 🔑 to say you did something wrong or that something bad is true
>
> **behave** (*verb*) 🔑 to do and say things in a particular way
>
> **boss** (*noun*) 🔑 a person at a workplace who tells other people what to do
>
> **fire** (*verb*) 🔑 to tell someone to leave his or her job
>
> **furniture** (*noun*) 🔑 tables, chairs, beds
>
> **punishment** (*noun*) 🔑 something bad that happens to someone because he or she did something wrong
>
> **reputation** (*noun*) what people say or think about someone or something
>
> **trouble** (*noun*) 🔑 a difficulty or problem

🔑 Oxford 2000 keywords

1. My grandparents have _____ with their loud neighbors.

2. These chairs are really old. I need some new _____.

3. Johnny, you were late. Your _____ is to stay after school.

4. Samantha never listens and doesn't follow company rules. I think we need to _____ her.

5. I'm sorry. I _____ that I made a mistake.

6. People say he is a very good worker and an honest person. He has an excellent _____.

7. Please stop telling me what to do all the time! You're not my _____!

8. We have visitors this weekend. Please be nice to them and _____ correctly.

B. Go online for more practice with the vocabulary.

C. PREVIEW Read each heading in the article. Who do you think is speaking in each situation? Write the heading number.

__2__ a. A child is speaking to a parent.

_____ b. A parent is speaking to a child.

_____ c. A sales clerk is speaking to a customer.

_____ d. One coworker is speaking to another coworker.

_____ e. A coworker is speaking to a manager.

_____ f. A friend is speaking to a group of friends.

_____ g. A husband is speaking to a wife.

_____ h. A classmate is speaking to another classmate.

D. QUICK WRITE Why do people lie? Write a list of possible reasons. Remember to use this section for your Unit Assignment.

WORK WITH THE READING

A. Read the article and gather information about if it is ever OK to lie.

The Lies People Tell

1   Most people don't **admit** it, but people often tell lies. These are eight lies people often tell.

Lie 1: "You look great!"

2   A woman asks her husband, "Does my hair look OK?" The husband doesn't like it, but he says something nice. He says, "You look great!" Why? He wants his wife to be happy. He doesn't want to hurt her feelings.

Lie 2: "I didn't do it!"

3   A boy breaks a cup. His mother asks, "Who broke the cup?" The boy says, "I didn't do it." Why? The boy did something wrong. He is afraid of the **punishment**. He tells a lie so he doesn't get in **trouble**.

"I didn't do it."

Lie 3: "He came to work on time."

4   Lina works in an office. Another worker in her office, Pete, has trouble with his car. Pete

often arrives late to work. The **boss** is not happy with him. The boss asks Lina, "Did Pete come to work on time today?" He didn't, but Lina says, "Yes." Why? She lies to protect him.

Lie 4: "The fish was three feet long!"

5   Joe is telling a story about his fishing trip. He says a fish he caught was three feet long, but it wasn't really very big. Why? He lies in order to tell a more interesting story.

Lie 5: "I can speak three languages."

6   Pamela tells her classmates, "I can speak three languages." She can really speak only two languages. Why does she lie? She wants to make a good impression[1] on her new classmates. Pamela wants them to think she is very intelligent.

Lie 6: "This special price is for today only."

7   A store ad says it has special prices on **furniture** for today only. The truth is that the price is the same every day. Why does the store lie? It lies in order to make more money. Customers buy more furniture when they believe the prices are special for one day only.

People tell lies for different reasons.

Lie 7: "His boss fired him from his last job!"

8   A man tells people at work that a new worker's boss **fired** him from his last job. This is not true. The man tells the lie to hurt the other worker's **reputation**.

Lie 8: "You will not get any gifts!"

9   A boy takes his little sister's toy. The parents say, "Give the toy back. You won't get any gifts for your birthday if you take your sister's toys." This is not true. The parents will give their son gifts for his birthday. Why do they lie? They lie to teach their son to **behave** better.

---

[1] **make a good impression:** to make people think good things about you

B. Circle the main idea of the article.

1. People do not admit they lie.

2. It is OK to lie.

3. People lie for different reasons.

4. People often tell lies.

C. Check (✓) the eight reasons people lie according to the article.

☑ We lie so we can sell more.

☑ We lie to hurt others.

☑ We lie to impress others.

☐ We lie to make funny jokes.

☑ We lie to make our stories more interesting.

☑ We lie to make people feel good.

☐ We lie to stay out of trouble.

☑ We lie to protect people we care about.

☐ We lie to relax.

☑ We lie to teach children to behave well.

D. Look back at your Quick Write on page 124. Why do people lie? Add any new information you learned from the article.

 **Tip** for Success

Make connections. Try to connect the information in the reading to new situations.

E. Read the statements. What kinds of lies are these? Write the lie number from the article next to each statement.

<u>5</u> 1. "I have traveled all over the world."

<u>7</u> 2. "I hear he never does his homework. He copies from everyone."

___ 3. "It wasn't me."

___ 4. "Ms. Watts is in a meeting. Can I take a message?"

___ 5. "The joke was so funny. We laughed all night."

___ 6. "This dinner is delicious!"

___ 7. "You are a special customer."

<u>8</u> 8. "Your thumbs will fall off if you text too much."

Dinner was delicious!

WRITE WHAT YOU THINK

A. Is it OK to tell these lies? Check *OK* or *Not OK* for each lie from Reading 1. Compare your answers in a group.

	OK	Not OK
1. "You look great!"	☐	☐
2. "I didn't do it!"	☐	☐
3. "He came to work on time."	☐	☐
4. "The fish was three feet long!"	☐	☐
5. "I can speak three languages."	☐	☐
6. "This special price is for today only."	☐	☐

The fish was three feet long!

B. Choose one question and write a response. Look back at your Quick Write on page 124 as you think about what you learned.

1. What is one lie from the chart in Activity A that you feel is OK? Why do you think so?

2. What is one lie from the chart in Activity A that you feel is not OK? Why do you think so?

Lie from the chart: ____

Why is it OK or not OK? _____

_____

_____

_____

Pronouns take the place of nouns and avoid repetition.

- ✓ Brian says **he** is coming here tomorrow. (subject pronoun)
- ✗ Brian says **Brian** is coming here tomorrow.

- ✓ Brian says to call **him** this evening. (object pronoun).
- ✗ Brian says to call **Brian** this evening.

Here are the subject and object pronouns.

Subject Pronouns	Object Pronouns
I	me
you	you
he	him
she	her
it	it
we	us
they	them

To understand a pronoun, you need to identify the noun it refers to. The noun that a pronoun refers to is called its **referent**. Look for

- a noun that comes **before** the pronoun. (It may be in a different sentence.)
- a noun that **agrees with** the pronoun in gender and number (For example, *he* agrees with *brother*, *she* does not; *it* agrees with *book*, *they* does not.)

If there are two or more possibilities, use the context to help you decide.

My sisters like to bake cakes, but they don't enjoy eating **them**.

It does not make sense for *sisters* to be the object of the verb *eat*. In this sentence, *them* refers back to *cakes*.

Look at these examples.

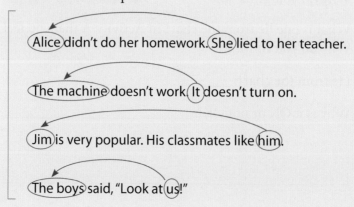

A. Read the sentences and look at the pronouns in bold. Circle the noun that the pronoun refers to.

1. People say **they** always tell the truth.

2. A small lie can grow big. **It** has a life of its own.

3. Children start to lie at age four or five. **They** lie to get out of trouble.

4. Janet lied about the schools she went to. **She** said she went to very famous schools.

5. Writer Stephen Glass lied in his stories. He lied to make **them** more interesting.

B. Read the excerpts from Reading 1 and look at the pronouns in bold. Then circle the noun that each pronoun refers to.

1. A woman asks her husband, "Do you like my hair?" The husband doesn't like **it**, but **he** says, "You look great!" Why? He wants **her** to be happy.
   a. **it:** woman / hair / husband
   b. **he:** woman / hair / husband
   c. **her:** woman / hair / husband

2. Lina works in an office. Another worker in her office, Pete, often has trouble with his car. The boss is not happy with **him**. **He** asks Lina, "Did Pete come to work on time today?" Lina says, "Yes." Why? **She** wants to protect him.
   a. **him:** Lina / Pete / boss
   b. **He:** Lina / Pete / boss
   c. **She:** Lina / Pete / boss

3. Pamela wants to make a good impression on her new classmates. Pamela wants **them** to think that **she** is very intelligent.
   a. **them:** the classmates / Pamela
   b. **she:** the classmates / Pamela

4. A boy takes his little sister's toy. The parents say, "Give **it** back. You won't get any gifts for your birthday if you take your sister's toy." This is not true. **They** will give **him** gifts for his birthday.
   a. **it:** the toy / the boy / the parents
   b. **They:** the toy / the boy / the parents
   c. **him:** the toy / the boy / the parents

 C. Go online for more practice identifying pronoun referents.

READING 2 | Honesty and Parenting

You are going to read an Internet forum about parenting. Use the Internet forum to gather information and ideas for your Unit Assignment.

PREVIEW THE READING

Vocabulary Skill Review

You learned in Unit 1 that some words are both nouns and verbs. They look the same but work differently in a sentence. Look up the words *avoid, practice, respect,* and *trust.* Which word is a verb only? Which words are also nouns?

A. **VOCABULARY** **Here are some words from Reading 2. Read the sentences. Then write each underlined word next to the correct definition.**

1. The <u>purpose</u> of this activity is to learn new words.

2. I don't agree with your <u>opinion</u>. You think it's OK to lie, but I don't.

3. You can <u>trust</u> him. He never lies.

4. I <u>respect</u> my father very much. I want to be like him.

5. Jill and Rob have a good <u>relationship</u>. They take care of each other.

6. Good football players <u>practice</u> every day.

7. People <u>require</u> eight hours of sleep a night. With less than eight hours of sleep, people get sick more often.

8. I try to <u>avoid</u> dangerous situations. That's why I don't go out after 11:00 at night.

a. _____ (*verb*) to think good things about someone

b. _____ (*verb*) to need something

c. _____ (*verb*) to try *not* to do something

d. _____ (*verb*) to believe that someone or something is honest and good and will not hurt you in any way

e. _____ (*verb*) to do something many times so that you will do it well

f. _____ (*noun*) what you think about something

g. _____ (*noun*) the reason for doing something

h. _____ (*noun*) the way people or groups feel about each other

 B. Go online for more practice with the vocabulary.

Oxford 2000 keywords

C. **PREVIEW** Look at the postings on the Internet forum. How many people respond to Marisa's question?

D. **QUICK WRITE** Do parents ever lie to their children? What kinds of lies do they tell? Remember to use this section for your Unit Assignment.

WORK WITH THE READING

A. Read the Internet forum and gather information about if it is ever OK to lie.

Honesty and Parenting

Marisa

Is it ever OK for a parent to lie to a child? My 10-year-old son plays soccer. He's not very good, but he loves it. Yesterday he played very badly. When he finished the game, he said, "Did I play well?" I said, "Yes! You're a great soccer player!" Did I do the right thing?

Bay212

Yes, you did the right thing. You told your son a white lie[1]. Your **purpose** was to make him feel good. Now he's ready to play soccer again.

Bernie

In my **opinion**, you should be honest. Your son wanted to know the truth. He knew he didn't play well. In time, he will learn not to believe you. He will not **trust** you. He will not **respect** you. Honesty is the first step to a good parent-child **relationship**.

Missy

You lied to make your son feel better, but you missed an opportunity to teach him a life lesson. People need to work hard for what they want. Maybe next time you can say, "No, you didn't play well today. Great soccer players **practice** a lot. Let's go practice." The truth will make him strong and a good soccer player.

Pixie

What do you say to him when he plays a good game? Do you lie and say that he is a really great player so he believes you? Every lie **requires** five more lies.

---

[1] **white lie:** a small lie that doesn't cause any harm

HueyBoy You worry too much. White lies are a necessary part of life. We need to lie to **avoid** hurting each other.

Linda I don't think there is ever a good reason to lie to our children. I want my children to become honest adults. Children learn honesty from the examples they see. We need to be honest in order to teach honesty to our children.

Parviz Children need honesty from their parents. Parents need to avoid lying, but they don't need to tell the whole truth. Next time, when your son asks, "Did I play well?" you can say, "What do you think?" Then your son can tell you what he thinks. That way, everything you say is true, and you avoid truth that hurts.

B. Read the statements. Write *T* (true) or *F* (false). Then correct the false statements.

_____ 1. Marisa is a grandmother.

_____

_____ 2. Marisa's son loves to play soccer.

_____

_____ 3. He is a great soccer player.

_____

_____ 4. He played a bad game.

_____

_____ 5. He asked if he played well.

_____

_____ 6. Marisa lied to her son.

_____

_____ 7. Marisa told her son that he had a bad game.

_____

C. Complete the chart with each person's opinion. Check (✓) *Yes* or *No*.

Is it OK for Marisa to lie to her son about his soccer ability?	Yes	No
1. Bay212	☐	☐
2. Bernie	☐	☐
3. Missy	☐	☐
4. Pixie	☐	☐
5. HueyBoy	☐	☐
6. Linda	☐	☐
7. Parviz	☐	☐

D. Look at Reading 2. Why is it OK for Marisa to lie? Why is it not OK? Write the reasons in the chart.

Children learn honesty from example.
Every lie requires more lies.
Honesty builds a strong relationship.
It's OK to lie to avoid hurting a person we love.
The lie gives the child the strength to try again.
The mother might lose her son's respect and trust.
Truth will make the child stronger.
White lies are necessary.

Reasons It's OK to Lie	Reasons It's Not OK to Lie

E. Discuss the questions in a group.

1. Which person in Reading 2 do you agree with? Why?

2. Which person in Reading 2 do you disagree with? Why?

F. Go online to read *Dishonest Journalism* and check your comprehension.

 WRITE WHAT YOU THINK

A. Discuss the questions in a group. Look back at your Quick Write on page 131 as you think about what you learned.

1. What kinds of lies do parents sometimes tell their children?

2. Which lies are OK to tell children?

 B. Go online to watch the video about lying in job interviews. Then check your comprehension.

C. Think about the unit video, Reading 1, and Reading 2 as you discuss the three quotations about honesty. What do you think they mean? Choose one quotation and write a response.

a. "When you tell the truth, you don't have to remember anything."

b. "A lie may take care of the present, but it has no future."

c. "A half-truth is a whole lie."

Quotation: _____

My response: _____

_____

_____

Vocabulary Skill | **Collocations**

 **Tip for Success**

You can use a collocations dictionary to help you learn common collocations. You can also find collocation information in most dictionaries.

Collocations are words that often go together.

✓ make the bed   ✓ do the dishes
✗ do the bed   ✗ make the dishes

In the examples, *do the bed* and *make the dishes* are possible grammatically, but speakers do not use these words together. *Make the bed* and *do the dishes* are the collocations that we use. Learning common collocations will help you speak and write more naturally.

A. Complete each collocation with a word or phrase from the box. These collocations are in Readings 1 and 2.

a good impression	someone's feelings
a lie	the right thing
a story	the truth
in trouble	

1. tell _____

2. tell _____

3. tell _____

4. make _____

5. do _____

6. hurt _____

7. get _____

B. Complete each sentence with a word or phrase from the box.

a good impression	stories	trouble
feelings	the right thing	truth

1. He lies so often. I never know when he is telling me the

   _____.

2. I'm sorry I lied. I didn't want to hurt your _____.

3. Sometimes it's hard to do _____, but it's

   important to try.

4. Jim tells funny _____. I always laugh when he

   tells the one about the fish.

5. My parents know I lied. I really don't want to get in

   _____.

6. She answered the boss's questions very well. She made

   _____.

 C. Go online for more practice with collocations.

WRITING

At the end of this unit, you will write an opinion paragraph about the importance of honesty. Your paragraph will include specific information from the readings and your own ideas.

Writing Skill Writing concluding sentences

A good **concluding sentence** closes the paragraph. Sometimes it tells the reader the main idea again.

> Sometimes we lie for good reasons. We lie to make people feel good. We lie to make our stories more interesting. We lie to protect the people we love. **There are times when a lie is better than the truth.**

Note: Concluding sentences are important in long paragraphs. Sometimes, concluding sentences are not necessary in short paragraphs.

A. **WRITING MODEL** Complete each model paragraph with the correct concluding sentence from the box.

> Every day, people lie to get out of trouble.
> It's OK to lie if it makes someone feel good.
> ~~Only truth can protect the people we love.~~
> When a person avoids the truth, the person is lying.

1. Some lies seem OK, but they can hurt people in the end. We tell these small lies to make people happy. We tell these lies to protect the people we love. In the end, the truth always comes out. In the end, the people we love are hurt and unhappy.

    Only truth can protect the people we love.

2. Sometimes people lie to avoid punishment. Sometimes a fast driver lies to avoid a ticket from a police officer. Sometimes an employee lies to avoid trouble with the boss. Sometimes a friend lies to avoid making a friend angry.

    _____

3. A half-truth is a whole lie. For example, a wife wants to go on a family vacation. The husband asks, "Can we pay for this vacation?" The wife knows it is very expensive, but she says, "Yes, we can pay for it." She's thinking, "We can pay for it with credit cards." She doesn't explain the whole truth.

_____

4. The only bad lies are the lies that hurt. Some people like to believe lies. They know the lies are not true, but they like to think they are. For example, someone says, "You make the best cup of coffee in the world." That probably isn't true, but it feels good to hear.

_____

B. Choose the best concluding sentence for each paragraph.

1. It's important to tell the truth to your children so that they learn to be honest. Children learn from watching their parents. If they see their parents telling lies—even white lies, they are more likely to think that lying is OK.
   a. Parents should provide a good example to their children by always telling the truth.
   b. Parents should also learn from watching their children.

2. How can you tell when someone is lying to you? Sometimes a person's body language can give you clues. Someone who is lying may not look you in the eye. Some people touch their mouth or nose when they're lying.
   a. Other people touch behind their ears.
   b. Body language can sometimes tell you more than words alone.

3. "Pinnochio" is an old story about a little boy who tells lies. In the story, every time Pinnochio tells a lie, his nose grows longer. His nose gets very long. At the end of the story, he learns to tell the truth.
   a. "Pinnochio" is a story with a simple message—don't lie.
   b. His nose gets small again.

C. Write a concluding sentence for each paragraph. Then read your sentences to a partner.

1.   Honesty is always the right way. Some people say that if the purpose of the lie is good, then the lie is OK. I don't think so. To have a good relationship, you need to respect and trust a person. It's not possible to trust and respect someone who lies.

_____

_____

2.   I have a good friend named Alex. He is very honest with me. If I make a mistake, he tells me. I always know he will tell me the truth. I trust him.

_____

_____

3.   It's important to be honest, but it's also important to be kind. Sometimes we have to make a decision between the two. In situations when the truth can hurt, I think it is better to say nothing.

_____

_____

4.   I believe white lies help us get along with others. For example, your friend shows you a photograph of her children. They are not good looking at all, but you tell a white lie. You tell your friend that her children are lovely. Your friend feels good. You feel good. What is the purpose of telling her that her children are unattractive?

_____

_____

D. Write a topic sentence and a concluding sentence for each paragraph.

1. Topic Sentence: _____

   _____

   First of all, it is not your responsibility that your co-worker is late. Your co-worker needs to take responsibility for his own actions. Secondly, your lies do not help your coworker solve the problem. Instead, you are helping your coworker avoid a solution. Finally, if the boss finds out you lied, she will not likely trust you later. You will hurt an important relationship.

   Concluding Sentence: _____

   _____

2. Topic Sentence: _____

   _____

   First of all, it is not fair to the employer. You are saying you have skills and experiences that you do not have. Secondly, it is not fair to the other applicants. Your lie gives you a special advantage. Finally, it is dangerous to lie on your résumé. If the company finds out you lied, they will likely fire you.

   Concluding Sentence: _____

   _____

In my last job I was in charge of three teams.

 E. Go online for more practice with writing concluding sentences.

Infinitives to show purpose

As you learned in the Unit 1 Grammar skill on page 18, an infinitive is *to* + the base form of the verb, and it can come after the verbs *like*, *want*, and *need*. Another way you can use an infinitive is to give a purpose for someone's action. An **infinitive of purpose** explains why someone does something.

> She lies to her child **to be** nice. (Why does she lie? Her purpose is to be nice.)
> They lied **to make** more money. (Why did they lie? Their purpose was to make more money.)
> They watch TV **to relax**. (Why do they watch TV? Their purpose is to relax.)
> We laugh **to improve** our health. (Why do we laugh? Our purpose is to improve our health.)

In order + infinitive to show purpose

You can also use *in order* + an infinitive to show the purpose. The meaning is the same, but it's more formal. Use *in order* with negative infinitives.

> She lies to her child **in order to be** nice.
> She lies to her child **in order not to hurt** his feelings.

A. Look back at Reading 1. Underline all the examples of infinitives of purpose. Write the number of examples of each. Compare your results with a partner.

1. There are ____ examples of infinitives of purpose in Reading 1.

2. There are ____ examples of *in order* + infinitive in Reading 1.

B. Complete each sentence. Use an infinitive of purpose or *in order* + infinitive and a reason from the box.

get out of trouble	make his friend feel good	protect his friend
hurt his friend	make money	

Tip for Success

A quotation mark introduces the exact words a person said. Use a comma after the verbs *say*, *tell*, etc.

1. Dennis didn't do his homework. The teachers asked him for his homework. Dennis said, "I did it, but I left it at home on my desk."

   Dennis lied _to get out of trouble_____.

2. A used car salesman said, "This car is in perfect condition." But the car has some serious problems.

   The salesman lied _____.

3. Jim is often in trouble in school. One day in class Jim broke a chair. The teacher asked the class, "Who broke this chair?" Jim's friend Gino said, "I did. I'm sorry. It was an accident."

   Gino lied _____.

4. John bought a ring for his mother. He showed the ring to his friend Sam. Sam thought it was ugly. Sam said, "The ring is beautiful. Your mother will love it."

   Sam lied _____.

5. Alex told Samir, "Nobody likes you." In fact, everyone likes Samir. Alex wants to be popular, too, but he isn't.

   Alex lied _____.

This car is in perfect condition.

 C. Go online for more practice with infinitives of purpose.

D. Go online for the grammar expansion.

In this assignment, you are going to write an opinion paragraph about the importance of honesty. As you prepare to write, think about the Unit Question, "Is it ever OK to lie?" Use information from Reading 1, Reading 2, the unit video, and your work in this unit to support your paragraph. Refer to the Self-Assessment checklist on page 144.

iQ ONLINE Go to the Online Writing Tutor for a writing model and alternate Unit Assignments.

PLAN AND WRITE

A. BRAINSTORM Complete the activities.

1. Read the question from the website LiarsHelpGroup.com.

> **Chad Chat:** I spend a lot of time on the Internet. I go to many Internet forums and talk with many people online. I don't give my real name. I have an online name. Sometimes I also tell small lies about myself. It's fun. I feel like a different person. Is it OK to lie online?

2. Discuss these questions with a partner.
   a. Why do you think Chad Chat lies about himself online?
   b. Is it OK to lie about yourself online?

3. Discuss the reasons in the chart with your partner. Then write two new possible reasons.

Reasons it's OK to lie online	Reasons it's not OK to lie online
People don't know who you are.	You can get in trouble.

B. **PLAN** Complete the outline with your opinion of the importance of honesty. Give reasons and details to support your opinion.

Topic sentence: _____

_____

1. **Reason 1:** _____

_____

Detail: _____

_____

2. **Reason 2:** _____

_____

Detail: _____

_____

3. **Reason 3:** _____

_____

Detail: _____

_____

4. **Concluding sentence:** _____

_____

C. **WRITE** Use your **PLAN** notes to write your paragraph. Go to *iQ Online* to use the Online Writing Tutor.

1. Write a clear topic sentence and details that support your opinion. Make sure your concluding sentence closes your paragraph or states your main idea again.

2. Look at the Self-Assessment checklist on page 144 to guide your writing.

REVISE AND EDIT

A. **PEER REVIEW** Read your partner's paragraph. Then go online and use the Peer Review worksheet. Discuss the review with your partner.

B. **REWRITE** Based on your partner's review, revise and rewrite your paragraph.

C. **EDIT** Complete the Self-Assessment checklist as you prepare to write the final draft of your paragraph. Be prepared to hand in your work or discuss it in class.

	SELF-ASSESSMENT	
Yes	**No**	
☐	☐	Circle the pronouns in your paragraph. Do they agree with their referents?
☐	☐	Does your concluding sentence remind the reader of your main idea?
☐	☐	Did you use collocations to make your writing sound natural?
☐	☐	Did you use infinitives of purpose to explain your reasons?
☐	☐	Does the paragraph include vocabulary from the unit?
☐	☐	Do you have both simple and compound sentences with *but* or *so*?
☐	☐	Did you use the words *because* and *when* correctly to explain reasons?
☐	☐	Is the spelling correct? Check a dictionary if you are not sure.
☐	☐	Does every sentence begin with a capital letter and end with final punctuation?

D. **REFLECT** Go to the Online Discussion Board to discuss these questions.

1. What is something new you learned in this unit?

2. Look back at the Unit Question—Is it ever OK to lie? Is your answer different now than it was when you started the unit? If yes, how is it different? Why?

TRACK YOUR SUCCESS

Circle the words you have learned in this unit.

<table>
<tr><td>

Nouns
boss 🔑
furniture 🔑
opinion 🔑
punishment 🔑
purpose 🔑
relationship 🔑
reputation
trouble 🔑

</td><td>

Verbs
admit 🔑
avoid 🔑
behave 🔑
fire 🔑
practice 🔑
require 🔑 AWL
respect 🔑
trust 🔑

</td></tr>
</table>

🔑 Oxford 2000 keywords
AWL Academic Word List

Check (✓) the skills you learned. If you need more work on a skill, refer to the page(s) in parentheses.

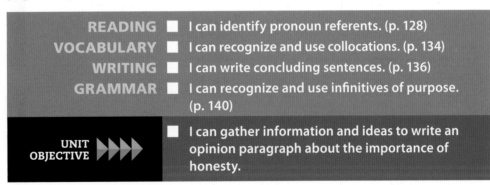

READING ■	I can identify pronoun referents. (p. 128)
VOCABULARY ■	I can recognize and use collocations. (p. 134)
WRITING ■	I can write concluding sentences. (p. 136)
GRAMMAR ■	I can recognize and use infinitives of purpose. (p. 140)
UNIT OBJECTIVE ▶▶▶▶ ■	I can gather information and ideas to write an opinion paragraph about the importance of honesty.

UNIT 7

READING ▶ marking the margins
VOCABULARY ▶ using the dictionary
GRAMMAR ▶ clauses with *after* and *after that*
WRITING ▶ making a timeline to plan your writing

Behavioral Science

UNIT QUESTION

How are children and adults different?

A Discuss these questions with your classmates.

1. At what age does a person become an adult?

2. Are you an adult?

3. Look at the photo. What is the child doing? How is he acting like an adult?

B Listen to *The Q Classroom* online. Then complete the chart.

a. ~~are logical~~	d. learn easily
b. change moods quickly	e. understand life better
c. have good imaginations	

Children	Adults
	a. are logical

 C Go to the Online Discussion Board to discuss the Unit Question with your classmates.

UNIT
OBJECTIVE ▶▶▶▶ Read the articles. Gather information and ideas to write
a paragraph about important changes in your life.

D Answer the questions. In a group of three, discuss your answers. Report your results to the class. Write *Y* (yes) or *N* (no) to record each answer. Then discuss the results with your group.

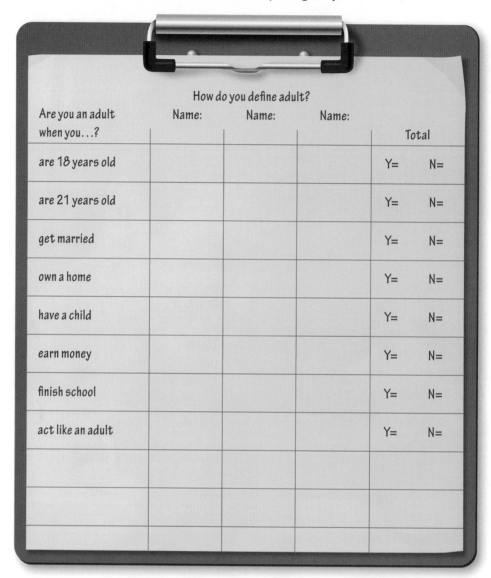

How do you define adult?

Are you an adult when you…?	Name:	Name:	Name:	Total
are 18 years old				Y= N=
are 21 years old				Y= N=
get married				Y= N=
own a home				Y= N=
have a child				Y= N=
earn money				Y= N=
finish school				Y= N=
act like an adult				Y= N=

E Discuss the photos with your group. Do any of the photos change your idea of an adult? Why or why not?

READING

READING 1 | What Is an Adult?

You are going to read an excerpt from a sociology textbook. It discusses what it means to be an adult. Use the reading to gather information and ideas for your Unit Assignment.

PREVIEW THE READING

Vocabulary Skill Review

In Unit 4, you learned about using the dictionary to identify the part of speech of a word. Use a dictionary to find the part of speech for each of these related words.

define (verb)

definition _____

grown (adjective)

grow _____

A. VOCABULARY Here are some words from Reading 1. Read their definitions. Then complete each sentence.

> **define** *(verb)* to say what a word means
>
> **grown** *(adjective)* 🔑 with the body of an adult; not a child
>
> **judgment** *(noun)* 🔑 your ability to make good decisions
>
> **legal** *(adjective)* 🔑 able to be done according to the laws of the government
>
> **organize** *(verb)* 🔑 to plan or arrange something
>
> **permission** *(noun)* 🔑 the action of giving someone the ability to do something
>
> **responsibility** *(noun)* 🔑 a duty to take care of someone or something
>
> **right** *(noun)* 🔑 what you can do, especially according to the law
>
> **vote** *(verb)* 🔑 to choose someone or something formally

🔑 Oxford 2000 keywords

1. This chart will help you _____ your ideas for writing.

2. Most children can't always make good choices because they don't have good _____.

3. I'm 75 years old. All of my children are _____.

4. In the United States, people _____ for a president every four years.

5. In most countries, it isn't _____ to get married at age 15.

6. You cannot leave the school without _____ from a teacher.

7. What does the word *adult* mean? Can you please _____ it?

8. All children have the _____ to an education.

9. Taking care of children is an important _____ .

iQ ONLINE **B.** Go online for more practice with the vocabulary.

Reading Skill | Marking the margins

Good readers think about the text as they read. They are active readers. One way to become an active reader is to **mark the margins**. The margins are the white space on each side of a text. Make marks in the margins when you find something interesting, when you read something you don't understand, and when you agree or disagree with the text.

Here are some marks you can use:

? = I don't understand.   **✓** = I agree.
! = That's interesting!   **✗** = I don't agree.

A. Read the paragraph. Then look at the marks the reader made and answer the questions.

bullet ant

There is a group of people in the Brazilian Amazon jungle called the Satere Mawé. When boys are ready to become men, they go through a difficult ritual[1]. The older men find many
? dangerous insects called bullet ants. Each ant's sting is much more painful than a bee sting. The older men put these ants inside special gloves. The
! boys must put their hands inside the gloves for ten minutes. The ants sting the boys' hands. The boys must do this twenty times over several years. The
✓ Satere Mawé believe that men must know how to handle painful situations in life. They believe this ritual teaches boys that lesson.

1. What does the reader not understand? _____

2. What does the reader think is interesting? _____

3. What does the reader agree with? _____

B. Mark the margins of Reading 1 as you read.

iQ ONLINE **C.** Go online for more practice marking the margins.

---

[1] **ritual:** a process that is planned and is repeated the same way every time

D. **PREVIEW** Read the article's headings. What are the four ways to define an adult?

1. _____

2. _____

3. _____

4. _____

E. **QUICK WRITE** How do you define an adult? Write a few sentences defining an adult in your own words. Remember to use this section for your Unit Assignment.

WORK WITH THE READING

A. Read the textbook excerpt and gather information about the differences between children and adults.

What Is an Adult?

1 How do you know when a person is an adult? Does the person's age tell you? Or is an adult a person who takes on **responsibility** for work and family? There are different ways to **define** an adult.

Age

2 One way to define an adult is by age, but countries have very different ideas about the **legal** age of an adult. In China, men can marry at age 22 and women at age 20. However, in Bolivia, the legal ages are 16 for men and 14 for women, with their parents' **permission**. In Brazil, a 16-year-old can **vote**, but in most African nations, people get this **right** at age 21. The legal driving age in Ethiopia is 14, and in Russia it is 18. The legal age of an adult is different around the world.

Body

3 Another way to define an adult is by the person's body. An adult is a person who is **grown** and can have children. This is a physical[1] definition of an adult. According to this definition, a 16-year-old is usually an adult.

Brain

4 Teenagers may have fully[2] grown bodies, but they don't usually think like adults. Their bodies usually stop growing at about age 17, but one part of the brain continues to grow until a person is about 25. This part of the brain, the frontal lobe, helps a person to understand cause and effect. It also helps a person to use good **judgment** to make decisions, solve problems, plan, and **organize**. When this part of the brain is fully grown at age 25, a person thinks like an adult. This is a psychological[3] definition of an adult.

[1] **physical:** relating to the body, not the mind
[2] **fully:** completely; totally

[3] **psychological:** connected to the mind or the way it works

Responsibilities

5   Another way of defining an adult is as a person who can take on important responsibilities like a job and a family. An adult respects others and understands that his or her own needs are not always the most important. This is the social[4] definition of an adult. Some teenagers behave like adults, but most are not that responsible until they are over 20 years old.

What Is an Adult?

6   There is no one moment when a person becomes an adult. Teenagers don't usually act or think like adults, but they begin to learn about adult responsibility. With each new responsibility (driving, working, voting, and having a family), a person comes closer to being a full adult. Most people agree that by age 25 a person is a full adult.

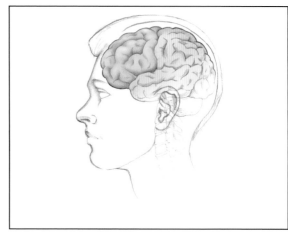

The frontal lobe of the brain

[4] **social:** connected with people who live in a place and the way they live together

B. Circle the main idea of the textbook excerpt.

1. An adult is a person who has a job.

2. A person becomes an adult at age 18.

3. There are different ways to define an adult.

4. Teenagers don't always think or act like adults.

C. Circle the answer that best completes each statement.

1. A man in China can marry when he is _____ years old.
    a. 16
    b. 18
    c. 22

2. People in Brazil can vote when they are _____.
    a. 16
    b. 18
    c. 22

3. People can get a driver's license in Ethiopia when they are _____ years old.
   a. 14
   b. 16
   c. 18

4. The human brain does not stop growing until a person is about _____ years old.
   a. 18
   b. 21
   c. 25

D. Read the different definitions of *adult*. Write the correct word from the box next to each definition in the chart.

legal	physical	psychological	social

1. _____	An adult is a person who: uses good judgment. can make decisions and solve problems. can plan and organize.
2. _____	An adult is a person who: respects others. understands others' needs. takes on responsibilities like family and work.
3. _____	An adult is a person who: can drive a car. can vote. can marry.
4. _____	An adult is a person: whose body is fully grown. who can have children.

E. The textbook excerpt says, "Teenagers may have fully grown bodies, but they don't usually think like adults." Do you agree? Do you disagree? Why?

F. Look back at your Quick Write on page 151. Add new information you learned from the reading. Has your definition of an adult changed?

WRITE WHAT YOU THINK

A. Look at your marks in the margin of Reading 1. Discuss the questions in a group.

1. Which ideas in Reading 1 do you not understand? Ask your classmates to explain them.

2. Which ideas in Reading 1 did you mark as interesting (!)? Why are they interesting to you?

3. Which ideas in Reading 1 did you agree (✓) or disagree (✗) with? Give your reasons.

B. Choose one of the questions above and write a response. Look back at your Quick Write on page 151 as you think about what you learned.

Question: ____

My response: _____

_____

_____

_____

_____

READING 2 | Becoming an Adult

You are going to read postings on the *Across the World* magazine blog. The magazine asked readers to post stories from their countries. Use the postings to gather information and ideas for your Unit Assignment.

PREVIEW THE READING

A. VOCABULARY Here are some words from Reading 2. Read the sentences. Then write each underlined word next to the correct definition.

1. All the students like to <u>participate</u> in the class discussion. It's a noisy class.

2. On this map, the colors green and blue <u>represent</u> land and water.

3. The teachers in our school <u>collect</u> our homework every day. That's why I always have it ready.

4. The family lived in a small <u>village</u>, but then they moved to a big city.

5. My brother loves to <u>dive</u> into the swimming pool. I don't know how to dive, so I prefer to jump into the water.

6. When you bungee jump, people <u>tie</u> elastic cords to your ankles.

7. Jamal attended his son's graduation <u>ceremony</u> at the university.

8. The 100 years from 1901 through 2000 are called the 20th <u>century</u>.

a. _____ *(verb)* to connect a cord or rope

b. _____ *(verb)* to take things from different people or places and put them together

c. _____ *(verb)* to do something together with other people

d. _____ *(verb)* to jump with your arms and head first, usually into water

e. _____ *(verb)* to be an example or sign of something

f. _____ *(noun)* a period of 100 years

g. _____ *(noun)* a formal public or religious event

h. _____ *(noun)* a very small town

iQ ONLINE **B.** Go online for more practice with the vocabulary.

C. PREVIEW Which country is each person from? Scan the postings and write the countries.

Tomas: _____

Pisiv: _____

Min Joo: _____

D. QUICK WRITE What important celebrations does your culture have for people between the ages of 15 and 21? Write a list of the celebrations. Remember to use this section in your Unit Assignment.

WORK WITH THE READING

A. Read the website and gather information about the differences between children and adults.

Across the World

Home　　　Log in

Becoming an Adult
Welcome to the *Across the World* Blog!

FRIDAY, AUGUST 3　　　　　　　　　　　COMMENTS 0

1　　*Across the World* magazine would like you to post your stories to our blog. What does becoming an adult mean in your country? Tell us your stories!

Becoming an Adult in Norway

SUNDAY, AUGUST 5　　　　　　　　　　COMMENTS 6

2　　My name is Tomas, and I live in Norway. In my country, there is a celebration called *Russ* when students finish high school. I **participated** in the *Russ* celebration this year. It began on May 1 and ended on May 17. We wore clothes that **represented** our studies in school; for example, I wore blue. All students who studied business wore blue. We wore blue clothes every day for 17 days. On the last day, we put on hats and walked in a parade[1]. At the end of the celebration, I was not a child anymore. I was an adult.

High school graduates in Norway enjoy their Russ celebration.

About

Links

Archives

January
February
March
April
May
June
July
August
September
October
November
December

---

[1] **parade:** an event in which people, cars, and trucks go down the street so that people can watch them

Becoming an Adult in the Republic of Vanuatu

MONDAY, AUGUST 6   COMMENTS 20

3 My name is Pisiv. I live on an island in the Republic of Vanuatu, in the
South Pacific Ocean. On my island, boys perform in an event called
Nanggol. When I was about to become a man, the men of my **village**
cut down trees and **collected** vines from the forest. They built a tall
tower of 25 meters. On a special day, I climbed to the top of the tower,
and the men **tied** long vines to my ankles. My family, friends, and
the people of the village watched and chanted. Then I **dived** head
first off the tower. My shoulders touched the ground when I landed.
That was important. Other boys in my village did it, too. Fortunately,
no one got hurt. After we returned to the village, we were men.

Becoming an Adult in Korea

WEDNESDAY, AUGUST 8   COMMENTS 36

4   I am from Korea. My name is Min Joo. I turned 19 years old this year, so
I participated in my country's coming-of-age[2] **ceremony**. The ceremony
started in the 10th **century**. At that time, the young prince[3] received new
adult clothes to show that he was not a child anymore. This celebration
became popular in the 14th century. In 1999, the government made the third
Monday in May, Coming-of-Age Day. Now all 19-year-olds participate in the
ceremony on that day. I wore a special Korean dress and walked with friends
to the ceremony. My family gave me flowers and many gifts. Now I am an
adult in Korea. I can drive, vote, and marry without my parents' permission.

[2] **coming-of-age:** when a person becomes an adult
[3] **prince:** the son of a king or queen

B. Read the statements. Write *N* (Norway), *RV* (Republic of Vanuatu), or *K* (Korea).

_____ 1. People here have a *Russ* celebration.

_____ 2. Only boys participate in the celebration in this country.

_____ 3. There is a celebration called *Nanggol* in this country.

_____ 4. The celebration in this country is for 19-year-olds.

_____ 5. The celebration here happens at the end of high school.

_____ 6. The celebration here is called Coming-of-Age Day.

C. Circle the answer that best completes each statement.

1. The *Russ* celebration in Norway is _____ long.
   a. one week
   b. two weeks
   c. more than two weeks

2. The colors of clothes in the *Russ* celebration represent students' _____.
   a. studies
   b. hats
   c. teachers

3. In the Republic of Vanuatu, boys dive off _____ when they are ready to become men.
   a. a vine
   b. a tower
   c. trees

4. The boys' _____ should touch the ground when they fall.
   a. head
   b. ankles
   c. shoulders

5. The first coming-of-age ceremony in Korea was in _____.
   a. the 10th century
   b. the 14th century
   c. the 20th century

6. A person becomes an adult in Korea at the age of _____.
   a. 18
   b. 19
   c. 20

D. **Look back at the reading on pages 156 and 157. Put the actions for each celebration in order.**

1. Russ Celebration (Number 1–4)

____ a. I put on a hat.

____ b. I walked in the parade with my classmates.

____ c. I was an adult.

__1__ d. I wore the color blue for 17 days.

2. Nanggol (Number 1–6)

____ a. I climbed to the top of the tower.

____ b. I dived off the tower to the ground.

____ c. I returned to the village as a man.

____ d. The village men built a tower with trees.

____ e. The village men tied a vine to my ankles.

____ f. My shoulders touched the ground.

3. Coming-of-Age Ceremony (Number 1–4)

____ a. I got the right to drive, vote, and marry.

____ b. I put on a Korean dress.

____ c. I walked with friends to the ceremony.

____ d. My family gave me flowers and gifts.

 E. **Go online to read** *Moving Back Home* **and check your comprehension.**

 # WRITE WHAT YOU THINK

A. Discuss the questions in a group.

1. What are other ceremonies that mark the change from child to adult? Look back at your Quick Write on page 155 as you think about what you learned.

2. Compare the celebrations you listed in your Quick Write to the celebrations described in the reading. How are they different? How are they similar?

B. Go online to watch the video about life coaches. Then check your comprehension.

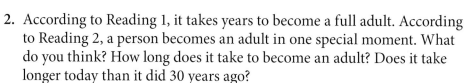

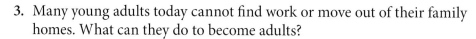

business plan (*n.*) a list of the things a business wants to do and how it will do them

goal (*n.*) something that you want to do in the future

graduate (*v.*) to finish school or university

life coach (*n.*) someone who helps people meet their goals

C. Think about the unit video, Reading 1, and Reading 2 as you discuss these questions.

1. What is the most important sign of being an adult? Why?

   - A coming–of–age ceremony
   - Driving a car
   - Finishing school
   - Getting a full-time job
   - Getting married
   - Having a child
   - Living independently from family
   - Voting

2. According to Reading 1, it takes years to become a full adult. According to Reading 2, a person becomes an adult in one special moment. What do you think? How long does it take to become an adult? Does it take longer today than it did 30 years ago?

3. Many young adults today cannot find work or move out of their family homes. What can they do to become adults?

Writing Tip

Remember to finish your paragraph with a concluding sentence.

D. Choose one question from Activity C and write a response.

Question: ____

My response: _____

_____

_____

_____

Words in a dictionary sometimes have more than one definition. Each definition has a number. It is important to know which definition you need. Here are some tips for **finding the correct definition**.

Tip for Success

Online dictionaries are also an excellent way to learn new vocabulary.

- Read the complete sentence. Is the word a *noun*, *verb*, *adjective*, or *adverb*?
- Look at the context, or other words in the sentence. They can sometimes give you information about the word you don't know.

In the example below, you can see that Definition 1 is the best definition for the word *gift* as it is used in the sentence below. The sentence refers to a gift that parents gave to their son. *Gift* can also mean "ability," but none of the words in the sentence discuss "ability," so Definition 2 does not make sense.

When he graduated, he received a wonderful **gift** from his parents.

gift ⚿ /gɪft/ *noun* [*count*]
1 something that you give to or get from someone: *This week's magazine comes with a special free gift.* ⊃ SYNONYM **present**
2 the natural ability to do something well: *She has a gift for languages.* ⊃ SYNONYM **talent**

All dictionary entries are from the *Oxford Basic American Dictionary for learners of English* © Oxford University Press 2011.

A. Read the sentences. Then write the number of the correct definition for each bold word.

col·lect¹ ⚿ /kəˈlɛkt/ *verb* (col·lect, col·lect·ing, col·lect·ed)
1 to take things from different people or places and put them together: *The teacher will collect the test booklets at the end of the exam.*
2 to bring together things that are the same in some way, in order to study or enjoy them: *My son collects stamps.*

_____ a. My brother **collects** toy cars. He has about 300 now.

_____ b. I **collected** all the library books in the house and returned them to the library.

re·spon·si·ble 🔑 /rɪˈspɑnsəbl/ *adjective*
1 having the duty to take care of someone or something: *The driver is **responsible for** the lives of the people on the bus.*
2 being the person who made something bad happen: *Who was **responsible for** the accident?*
3 A **responsible** person is someone that you can trust: *We need a responsible person to take care of our son.* ➔ ANTONYM **irresponsible**

____ c. Kelly is very **responsible**. She's only 15, but she has a job, and she is saving money for college.

____ d. I'm **responsible** for my younger brothers and sisters when we go to the park. I make sure they don't get hurt.

____ e. Jack was **responsible** for the fire. He forgot the stove was on.

Kelly is very responsible. She has a job, and she is saving money for college.

B. Look up each bold word in the dictionary. Find the correct definition and write it on the line. Pay attention to the part of speech.

1. Children need to learn the difference between **right** and wrong.

   right: _____

2. We sent the young man to **represent** our village at the meeting.

   represent: _____

3. The lawyer didn't agree with the **judgment**, but he did not say anything.

   judgment: _____

iQ ONLINE **C.** Go online for more practice with using the dictionary.

WRITING

At the end of this unit you will write a paragraph about important changes in your life from the past 5 or 10 years. Your paragraph will include specific information from the readings and your own ideas.

Grammar   Clauses with *after* and *after that*

You can use *after* or *after that* when you write about a series of events. The word *after* makes it clear to the reader that one thing happened first and then another thing happened.

After

After combines two sentences into one. It comes before the first event. It can either begin the sentence or come in the middle of the sentence.

first event | second event

After I got married, I moved out of my parents' house.

second event | first event

I moved out of my parents' house **after** I got married.

After that

Use *after that* to connect a second sentence to a first one. It comes in the second sentence and indicates a second event. It can come at the beginning or the end of the sentence.

first event | second event

I got my own passport at age 16. **After that**, I really felt like an adult.

first event | second event

I got my own passport at age 16. I really felt like an adult **after that**.

A. For each sentence or pair of sentences, circle the first event and underline the second event.

1. After (I turned 18,) I graduated from high school.

2. I moved to New York after I finished college.

3. I had my first child when I was 25. After that, I wanted another child.

4. After the coming-of-age ceremony, my friends and I celebrated.

5. After I voted for the first time, I felt like a responsible adult.

6. I learned how to drive after I turned 18.

B. Read the sentences. Write a sentence with *after* or two sentences with *after that*.

1. First event: We got married.

   Second event: My wife and I moved to California.

   (*after*) _____

2. First event: I went to my coming-of-age ceremony.

   Second event: I still didn't feel like a real adult.

   (*after*) _____

3. First event: I moved out of my parents' house when I was 19.

   Second event: I had a difficult time.

   (*after that*)_____

4. First event: I turned 16 last year.

   Second event: I started being more responsible.

   (*after that*)_____

C. Go back to Activity D on page 159. Connect sentences with *after* and *after that*.

Example: After I walked in the parade with my classmates, I was an adult.

   I walked in the parade with my classmates. After that, I was an adult.

D. Go online for more practice with clauses with *after* and *after that*.

E. Go online for the grammar expansion.

A **timeline** is a list of important events and the times that they happened. You can make a timeline to help you write a narrative—a story.

Here is a timeline of someone's perfect day.

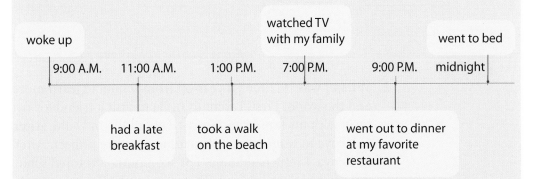

Here is a paragraph based on the timeline. Notice that you can add details to your paragraph that are not included in your timeline. Use your timeline only as a guide for your writing.

> I had a perfect day last Saturday. I woke up at 9:00 a.m. I read a book for a little while. Then I had a late breakfast at 11:00 a.m. At 1:00 p.m., I took a walk on the beach. It was a beautiful day. After that, I called a friend and invited her to dinner. At 7:00 p.m., I watched TV with my family, and at 9:00 p.m., my friend and I had dinner at my favorite restaurant. After dinner, I was really tired. I went to bed after midnight.

A. WRITING MODEL **Read the model paragraphs and complete the timelines on page 166.**

1. Last year I went to England to study. For the month of August, I studied at a four-week program. After that, I moved in with an English family. All September I had to speak English every day! In October I started classes at the college. I studied until the end of December. When school got out, I travelled around England. I visited many places and met many interesting people. During my time in England, I learned so much. In February I returned home as an adult.

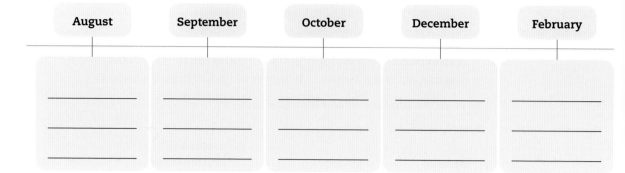

August	September	October	December	February
_____	_____	_____	_____	_____
_____	_____	_____	_____	_____
_____	_____	_____	_____	_____

2. When I was 19, I took a year off from school to learn more about myself and the world. First, I went to India to visit a friend for two months. I lived with his family and learned about life in Delhi. After that, I went to Kenya to work on an international nature project. After four months in Kenya, I returned home. For six months I tutored school children at my neighborhood school. That year I was off from school, but I learned a lot. After 12 months, I was ready to go back to school and study to become a doctor.

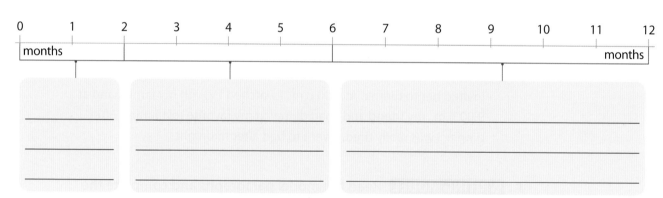

B. Read the timeline and write a paragraph. Remember to connect sentences with *after*, *after that*, and *when*. Look back at page 91 to review sentences with *when*.

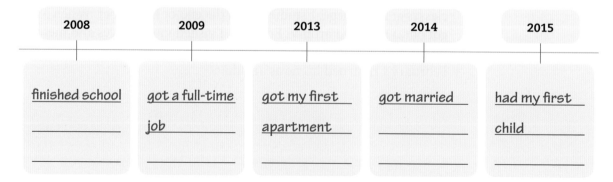

2008	2009	2013	2014	2015
finished school	got a full-time	got my first	got married	had my first
_____	job	apartment	_____	child
_____	_____	_____	_____	_____

Activity C asks you to **construct**, or make, a timeline about your perfect day. To make or construct something new, you have to put information together in a different way. This can help you understand your ideas better.

C. Look back at the Writing Skill box on page 165. Reread the paragraph about a perfect day. Make a timeline to show your perfect day. Write a short note about each important event. Then tell a partner about your day.

D. Write at least six sentences about your perfect day. Use your timeline, any other information you told your partner, and any other details you want to add.

 **E.** Go online for more practice with making a timeline to plan your writing.

Unit Assignment | Write a paragraph about important changes in your life

 In this assignment, you are going to write a paragraph about three to five important changes in your life in the past five to ten years. How is your life different now than it was ten years ago? As you prepare your paragraph, think about the Unit Question, "How are children and adults different?" Use information from Reading 1, Reading 2, the unit video, and your work in this unit to support your paragraph. Refer to the Self-Assessment checklist on page 168.

iQ ONLINE Go to the Online Writing Tutor for a writing model and alternate Unit Assignments.

PLAN AND WRITE

A. BRAINSTORM Write a list of events in your life that were important to you. Write for five minutes.

B. PLAN Complete the activities.

1. Choose four to six of the events you wrote about in Activity A. Put the events in order on a timeline. (Draw a timeline like the one you constructed in Activity A on page 166.)

2. Work with a partner. Tell your partner about the events on your timeline. Ask and answer questions about the events. Add any details to your timeline.

C. **WRITE** Use your **PLAN** notes to write your paragraph. Go to *iQ Online* to use the Online Writing Tutor.

Tip for Success

When you write your paragraph, remember to write three or more ideas that support your topic sentence and to write a concluding sentence.

1. Use the information from your timeline in Activity B to help you. You can use this topic sentence to begin your paragraph, or write your own: *Several experiences in my life were important.*

2. Look at the Self-Assessment checklist to guide your writing.

REVISE AND EDIT

A. **PEER REVIEW** Read your partner's paragraph. Then go online and use the Peer Review worksheet. Discuss the review with your partner.

B. **REWRITE** Based on your partner's review, revise and rewrite your paragraph.

C. **EDIT** Complete the Self-Assessment checklist as you prepare to write the final draft of your paragraph. Be prepared to hand in your work or discuss it in class.

SELF-ASSESSMENT		
Yes	No	
☐	☐	Does your paragraph begin with a topic sentence that introduces the events in your life?
☐	☐	Do your supporting sentences explain why the events were important to you?
☐	☐	Do you provide details to support your sentences?
☐	☐	Did you present the events in the order they occurred?
☐	☐	Does your concluding sentence remind readers of why the events are important?
☐	☐	Did you use *after*, *after that*, and *when* to help your readers understand the order of events?
☐	☐	Does your paragraph include vocabulary from the unit?
☐	☐	Did you check the paragraph for punctuation, spelling, and grammar?

D. **REFLECT** Go to the Online Discussion Board to discuss these questions.

1. What is something new you learned in this unit?

2. Look back at the Unit Question—How are children and adults different? Is your answer different now than when you started the unit? If yes, how is it different? Why?

TRACK YOUR SUCCESS

Circle the words you have learned in this unit.

Nouns	Verbs	Adjectives
century 🔑	collect 🔑	grown 🔑
ceremony 🔑	define AWL	legal 🔑 AWL
judgment 🔑	dive	
permission 🔑	organize 🔑	
responsibility 🔑	participate AWL	
right 🔑	represent 🔑	
village 🔑	tie 🔑	
	vote 🔑	

🔑 Oxford 2000 keywords

AWL Academic Word List

Check (✓) the skills you learned. If you need more work on a skill, refer to the page(s) in parentheses.

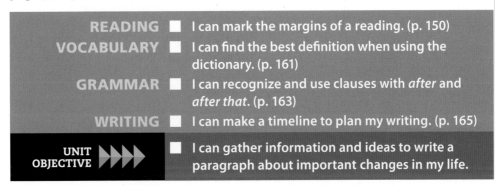

READING ☐	I can mark the margins of a reading. (p. 150)
VOCABULARY ☐	I can find the best definition when using the dictionary. (p. 161)
GRAMMAR ☐	I can recognize and use clauses with *after* and *after that*. (p. 163)
WRITING ☐	I can make a timeline to plan my writing. (p. 165)
UNIT OBJECTIVE ▶▶▶▶ ☐	I can gather information and ideas to write a paragraph about important changes in my life.

READING	▶	identifying facts and opinions
VOCABULARY	▶	word families
WRITING	▶	contrasting ideas with *however*
GRAMMAR	▶	comparative adjectives

UNIT QUESTION

What are you afraid of?

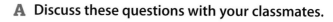

A Discuss these questions with your classmates.

1. When do you feel afraid?

2. What do you do to stay safe?

3. Look at the photos. Which of these would you be most afraid of? Why?

Read the articles. Gather information and ideas to write one or more paragraphs about a fear and explain how it can be avoided.

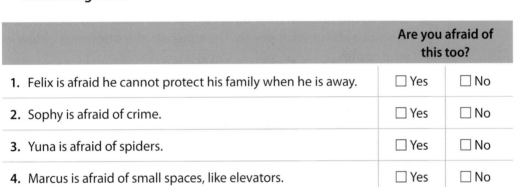

🔊 **B** Listen to *The Q Classroom* online. Then complete the chart. Compare answers with your classmates. Are your classmates afraid of these things too?

	Are you afraid of this too?	
1. Felix is afraid he cannot protect his family when he is away.	☐ Yes	☐ No
2. Sophy is afraid of crime.	☐ Yes	☐ No
3. Yuna is afraid of spiders.	☐ Yes	☐ No
4. Marcus is afraid of small spaces, like elevators.	☐ Yes	☐ No

 C Go to the Online Discussion Board to discuss the Unit Question with your classmates.

D For each statement, mark an ✘ on the line according to how you feel. Then compare your answers in a group.

	Strongly disagree	Strongly agree

1. The world is a dangerous place. ←——————————————→

2. I am afraid to be alone at night. ←——————————————→

3. I never talk to people I don't know. ←——————————————→

4. There are many dangerous people in the world. ←——————————————→

5. I wash my hands a lot so I don't get sick. ←——————————————→

6. The news on TV is scary. ←——————————————→

E Look at the photos. How does each photo make you feel? Write a sentence about each photo. Then discuss the questions below with your group.

lightning

snakes

flying

heights

1. Which photo do you fear the most? Why?

2. Which photo do you fear the least? Why?

3. Are your responses similar or different? In what ways?

READING

READING 1 | A Dangerous World?

UNIT OBJECTIVE ▶▶▶

You are going to read an article about crime and crime reporting. Use the article to gather information and ideas for your Unit Assignment.

PREVIEW THE READING

Tip for Success

People often misuse the words *affect* and *effect*. *Affect* (verb) means "to change." *Effect* (noun) means "the change that happens because of something." For example: *Crime affects us. The effects are fear and worry.*

A. **VOCABULARY** Here are some words from Reading 1. Read the sentences. Then write each <u>underlined</u> word next to the correct definition.

1. This neighborhood has a lot of <u>crime</u>. Be careful!

2. I don't like <u>violent</u> stories. I don't like to imagine people getting hurt.

3. Every day, there are many important news events in the world. However, our <u>focus</u> is often on sports stars or other famous people.

4. I read a <u>scary</u> story last night. I was so afraid I couldn't sleep!

5. Websites can <u>report</u> on news events more quickly than TV news.

6. Most people own a cell phone. Cell phones are <u>common</u> today.

7. Smoking can <u>affect</u> your health. It can make you sick.

8. Eating a lot of fast food can have a <u>negative</u> effect on your health.

a. _____ (*verb*) to give people information about something that happened

b. _____ (*verb*) to make something or someone change in a particular way, especially in a bad way

c. _____ (*noun*) the center of attention or interest

d. _____ (*noun*) something that someone does that is not legal

e. _____ (*adjective*) making you feel afraid

f. _____ (*adjective*) bad; not positive or good

g. _____ (*adjective*) happening often or found in many places

h. _____ (*adjective*) strong and dangerous; can hurt you

B. Go online for more practice with the vocabulary.

C. PREVIEW Look at the chart in the article. What does it tell you about crime from 2002 to 2012?

D. QUICK WRITE What do you think? Is there more crime today than there was ten years ago? Where do you learn about the crime rate? Remember to use this section for your Unit Assignment.

WORK WITH THE READING

A. Read the article and gather information on unreasonable fear and how it can be avoided.

A Dangerous World?

1   Is **crime** increasing in your town or city? In many places, crime rates are going down. The truth is that crime rates are much lower today than 20 years ago. Since 1993 crime has decreased 65 percent.

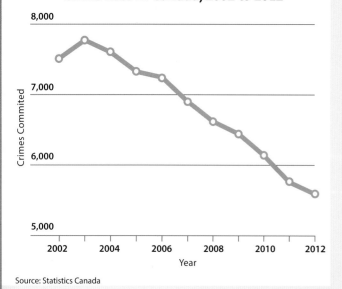

Crime Rate in Canada, 2002 to 2012

Source: Statistics Canada

Between 2002 and 2012, the rate of violent crime went down in Canada.

However, most people believe that crime rates are increasing. 68 percent of people say there is more crime this year than last year. They think that **violent** crime happens in their towns and cities all the time.

What makes people afraid?

2   The news media focuses on crime. The first story on the evening news is usually a story about violent crime. On some news programs over 40 percent of the news stories are about crime. Why is there such a **focus** on crime? It is because **scary** news programs are popular.

Does the media give people a true picture of the world?

3   No. The media does not give people a true idea of the level of danger in the world. Here is an interesting example. Between 2002 and 2012, the rate of violent crime went down in Canada. However, a study showed that during part of that time, news stories about violent crime increased from 10 to 25 percent. One year, almost 25 percent of the stories the

Canadian news **reported** were about gun crime, but only 3.3 percent of violent crime that year was gun crime.

4 The media's focus on crime gives people the wrong idea. People believe there is more crime than there really is. They think violent crime is common.

What are the effects of this exaggerated[1] focus on violent crime?

5 It **affects** people's lives in a **negative** way. This focus on violent crime results in increased feelings of fear. In order to protect themselves, some people avoid going out. They do not talk to their neighbors. As a result, they know and trust fewer people. They have fewer friends. This increases their fear about the dangers in the world.

6 Fear of crime can also affect people's health. Many parents keep their children inside their homes. They believe the world outside is too dangerous. The children don't walk, run, or play sports outside. They become less healthy. This is true for older adults too.

7 The media's focus on crime makes us believe the world is a scarier place than it is. It makes us lonelier and less happy and healthy. Facts show that we should learn to worry less. It's good to be careful and stay safe, but the world around us is actually safer than we think.

---

[1] **exaggerated:** bigger or worse than it really is

B. Circle the answer that best completes each statement according to Reading 1.

1. The crime rate is ___ in many places.
   a. going up
   b. the same
   c. going down

2. Most people think the crime rate is ___.
   a. going up
   b. the same
   c. going down

3. Canadian media made people believe that the crime rate was ___.
   a. going up
   b. the same
   c. going down

4. The media's focus on crime affects people in ___.
   a. positive ways
   b. negative ways
   c. exciting ways

C. Read paragraphs 1 and 2 again. Find the supporting information for the following statements.

1. The truth is crime rates are much lower today than 20 years ago. (Paragraph 1)

   Supporting fact: _____

   _____

2. Most people believe crime rates are increasing. (Paragraph 1)

   Supporting fact: _____

   _____

3. The news media focuses on crime. (Paragraph 2)

   Supporting fact: _____

   _____

D. Read Paragraph 3 again. Answer the questions.

1. Reality: Rate of violent crime went down.

   What did the media do?

   _____

2. Reality: 3.3 percent of violent crime was gun crime.

   What did the media do?

   _____

E. Read Paragraph 5 again. Put the information in the chart on page 177 in the correct order.

~~People are more afraid.~~

People avoid going out.

People know and trust fewer people.

People don't talk to neighbors.

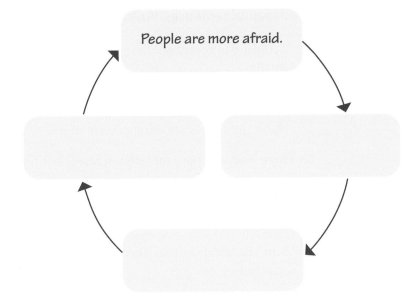

People are more afraid.

F. Answer this question: How does the media's focus on crime affect us?

_____

_____

Reading Skill | Identifying facts and opinions

A supporting sentence or detail in a text is usually either a **fact** or an **opinion**. Knowing the difference between a fact and an opinion is important for a reader. It can help you decide the purpose of a text and judge how well the author supports the ideas in the text.

Facts are things that you know happened or are true. Opinions are what you think or feel about something.

Here are some common words that tell you a statement is an opinion and not a fact.

- The verbs _think_ and _believe_ often introduce opinions.

  > I **think** violent TV programs are scary.
  > Some people **believe** violent TV programs cause more crime.

- The modal _should_ introduces the writer's opinion. (_Should_ goes before another verb. You use _should_ to tell someone what you think is or isn't a good idea.)

  > Television news **should** report more positive news.
  > Reporters **shouldn't** focus only on crime.

A. Read each pair of sentences. Write *F* (fact) or *O* (opinion).

1. ____ a. According to recent studies, crime rates are going down in Canada.

   ____ b. People believe crime rates are increasing.

2. ____ a. I think the streets are dangerous at night.

   ____ b. There was a robbery on Jackson Street last night.

3. ____ a. Children shouldn't watch violent programs on television.

   ____ b. By the age of 18, people see 200,000 violent crimes on television.

4. ____ a. Many studies show that violent news stories affect people in a negative way.

   ____ b. Some people believe that violent stories on the news make us more afraid.

B. Read Reading 1 again. Underline all the statements of opinion that use the words *think*, *believe*, and *should*.

 C. Go online for more practice identifying facts and opinions.

 ## WRITE WHAT YOU THINK

A. Discuss the questions in a group.

1. Do you watch the news on TV? Do you listen to the news on the radio? Do you read the news online or in a newspaper? Tell your group where you get the news and why (or why you don't get the news).

2. Do you think crime is going up or going down where you live? Explain your answer.

3. Are there differences in opinion between group members who watch the news on TV and those who read the news? Why do you think this is?

B. Choose one of the questions in Activity A and write a response. Look back at your Quick Write on page 174 as you think about what you learned.

Question: _____

My response: _____

_____

_____

_____

_____

READING 2 | ## Can We Trust Our Fears?

UNIT OBJECTIVE ▶▶▶▶

You are going to read an online article about human fears. Use the article to gather information and ideas for your Unit Assignment.

PREVIEW THE READING

Vocabulary Skill Review

In Unit 1, you learned that some words have the same form as a noun and a verb. Look up these words from this unit in your dictionary: *crime, fear, focus, harm,* and *report.* Do they all have a noun and verb form?

A. VOCABULARY Here are some words from Reading 2. Read their definitions. Then complete each sentence.

contain (*verb*) 🔑 to have something inside
death (*noun*) 🔑 when a life ends
disease (*noun*) 🔑 an illness or sickness
factor (*noun*) one of the things that can affect or change a decision, or a situation
fat (*noun*) 🔑 an oil we get from the plants, seeds, and animals we eat
frighten (*verb*) 🔑 to make someone feel afraid
harm (*verb*) 🔑 to hurt or damage someone or something
pleasure (*noun*) 🔑 the feeling of being happy or enjoying something
reasonable (*adjective*) 🔑 fair or right in a particular situation

🔑 Oxford 2000 keywords

1. My horse is big and strong, but he never tries to _____ anyone.

2. Stress is one _____ that can affect your health. Food is another.

3. I was sorry to hear about the _____ of your father. He was a wonderful man.

4. That's a _____ plan. I'm sure it will work out well.

5. Scary stories really _____ me!

6. The white part of the meat is the _____. I cut it off and don't eat it because it's not healthy.

7. My neighbor has a serious _____. He is in the hospital.

8. I love to go to nice restaurants. Eating there is a great _____ for me.

9. Our bodies _____ a lot of water—over 50 percent, in fact, is water.

iQ ONLINE **B. Go online for more practice with the vocabulary.**

C. **PREVIEW** Read the first paragraph of the article. What is the purpose of fear? What will the article tell us about fear?

D. **QUICK WRITE** What are your three biggest fears? Write a few sentences. Remember to use this section for your Unit Assignment.

WORK WITH THE READING

 A. Read the article and gather information about unreasonable fear and how it can be avoided.

Can We Trust Our Fears?

1   Are you more afraid of bird flu[1] or the common flu[2]? Which **frightens** you more, mad cow **disease**[3] or heart disease[4]? Fear is a natural human feeling. The purpose of fear is to protect us from things that **harm** us. However, we can't always trust our fears.

2   Sometimes we are afraid of things that are not likely to happen. Many people think bird flu is very dangerous, but we don't worry about the common flu. Only 360 people have ever died of the bird flu. However, every year 250,000 to 500,000 people die from the common flu. Many people are not afraid to eat unhealthy foods, but we're afraid of getting mad cow disease from beef. In fact, we are much more likely to get heart disease than mad cow disease. Heart disease is the number-one cause of **death** in the world. In 2008 alone, 17.5 million people died of heart disease. Fewer than 300 people, however, ever died of mad cow disease. Why are we more afraid of things that we are unlikely to ever experience? There are a few different **factors**.

3   First of all, when something is familiar to us or common in our experience, we fear it less. For example, most of us get the common flu several times in our lives.

We are more likely to get heart disease than mad cow disease.

However, we never get bird flu. We probably don't know anyone who had bird flu. Bird flu is unknown, so it's scarier.

4   Another factor is control. We are more afraid of things we cannot control. Mad cow disease is dangerous. It is very difficult to know if meat **contains** mad cow disease. Mad cow disease cannot be stopped by doctors. We have no control over it. Doctors can usually help people with heart disease, though. They can control it. And doctors believe people can fight heart disease. They say that we should exercise and eat less of some kinds of **fat**. We know we can control heart disease.

---

[1] **bird flu:** an illness humans can get from birds
[2] **common flu:** an illness many people get every year
[3] **mad cow disease:** an illness that kills cows and can kill people who eat beef from sick cows

[4] **heart disease:** any disease that causes the heart to stop working correctly

5 So why do we do things that we know are dangerous? If something gives us **pleasure**, we might continue to do it despite[5] the danger. For example, maybe your mother and your grandfather had heart disease. You know that you need to eat well, but you really like food with a lot of fat. So you eat it anyway. You say, "Someday I will change the way I eat, but I'm hungry and the unhealthy food is delicious."

6 Now, think about the things that you are afraid of. How likely are they to happen? Do you think your fears are **reasonable**? Think about your fears honestly, and you might be surprised. You may find out that you are living with unnecessary fears.

[5] **despite:** although something happened or is true

B. Read the statements. Write *T* (true) or *F* (false). Then correct the false statements to make them true. Where is the information found in the article? Write the paragraph number.

Paragraph #

____ 1. Unfamiliar things frighten us more. ____

_____

____ 2. We fear things we can control. ____

_____

____ 3. Fear is natural. ____

_____

____ 4. All of our fears are reasonable. ____

_____

____ 5. We are afraid of things that are unlikely to happen. ____

_____

____ 6. We may do things that harm us because we enjoy them. ____

_____

C. What are reasonable fears, according to the article? What are unreasonable fears? Write the words in the chart.

| fear of bird flu | fear of heart disease |
| fear of the common flu | fear of mad cow disease |

Reasonable Fears	Unreasonable Fears

D. Answer these questions.

1. Why are people more afraid of bird flu than the common flu?

_____

_____

2. Why are people more afraid of mad cow disease than heart disease?

_____

_____

3. Why are we afraid of things that are not dangerous?

_____

_____

4. Why do we do some things that <u>are</u> dangerous?

_____

_____

E. Go online to read *Crime in Our City* and check your comprehension.

 # WRITE WHAT YOU THINK

A. Discuss these questions in a group.

1. Look back at your Quick Write on page 180. What fears did you write about? Why do you think you have these fears?

2. Do you think your fears are reasonable or unreasonable? Why? Are they things you cannot control? Are they things that are unfamiliar? Are your fears likely to happen?

 B. Go online to watch the video about police in a small town. Then check your comprehension.

VIDEO VOCABULARY

budget *(n.)* a plan of how to spend money

police chief *(n.)* the leader of the police in a town or city

police officer *(n.)* a person who works in the police force

Writing **Tip**

Use both long and short sentences to make your writing more interesting. To make your sentences longer and more complex, connect sentences with words like *and, so, but, when*, or *because*.

C. Think about the unit video, Reading 1, and Reading 2 as you discuss the questions. Then choose one question and write a response.

1. In Reading 1 and Reading 2, you read that people sometimes fear things unnecessarily. What do you think people <u>should</u> be afraid of?

2. Write down all the fears that you have discussed so far in this unit. Which fears do you think are unreasonable? Explain your answer.

Question: ____

My response: _____

_____

_____

_____

A **word family** is a group of words that come from the same word. The bold words in the sentences are members of the same word family. Notice that they are each a different part of speech.

> Some people spend a lot of money on home **protection**. (noun)
> They want to **protect** their homes from criminals. (verb)
> They buy **protective** alarm systems for their homes. (adjective)

This chart shows two word families.

Noun	Verb	Adjective	Adverb
familiarity	familiarize	familiar	familiarly
pleasure	please	pleasant	pleasantly

When you learn a new word, also try to learn the other members of the word family. Learning word families can help build your vocabulary more quickly.

A. Complete the chart. Use your dictionary to help you.

	Noun	Verb	Adjective	Adverb
1.	fear	fear	fearful	fearfully
2.	violence			
3.			believable	
4.	danger	endanger		
5.			harmful	
6.	safety			

B. Complete each sentence with a word from the chart in Activity A.

1. We often _____ *fear* _____ the things we can't control.

2. We feel _____ in this neighborhood. We often go out at night to visit our neighbors.

3. The man hit the wall _____. He was very angry.

4. The news reports a lot of gun _____, but most crime isn't gun crime.

5. You may be in _____ if you travel alone at night.

6. I'm not afraid when Saad drives because he drives very _____.

7. Being afraid of the dark is a common _____.

iQ ONLINE   **C.** Go online for more practice with word families.

WRITING

At the end of this unit, you will write one or more paragraphs about an unreasonable fear and how it can be avoided. Your paragraph(s) will include specific information from the readings and your own ideas.

Writing Skill | Contrasting ideas with *however*

The word *however* introduces an idea that is different from, or contrasts with, the idea before it. *However* is similar in meaning to the word *but*.

> My neighborhood is dangerous, **but** it has many nice qualities.
> My neighborhood is dangerous. **However**, it has many nice qualities.

But is a *conjunction*. It connects two sentences into one. *However* is a *transition*. It links two sentences.

- *However* usually comes at the beginning of the second sentence. Use a comma after *however*.

> Crime rates are going down. **However**, most people think there is more crime.

- When you want the focus of the sentence to be about the subject, you can put *however* after the subject. Put commas before and after it.

> Crime rates are going down. Most people, **however**, think the world is more dangerous.

- When the contrast is less important, you can also put *however* at the end of the sentence. Place a comma before it.

> Crime rates are going down. Most people think there is more crime, **however**.

A. Here are some facts from Readings 1 and 2. Connect the sentences. Write the letter on the line.

____ 1. Crime rates are much lower today.

a. However, we never get bird flu.

____ 2. The purpose of fear is to protect us from things that harm us.

b. However, news stories about violent crime increased from 10 to 25 percent.

____ 3. Only 360 people ever died of the bird flu.

c. However, most people believe that crime is increasing.

____ 4. The rate of violent crime went down in Canada.

d. However, we can't always trust our fears.

____ 5. Most of us get the common flu several times in our lives.

e. However, every year up to 500,000 people die from the common flu.

B. Connect the sentences with *however* in three different ways.

1. People wash their hands for about 9 seconds. It takes 15 seconds to kill the germs.

   <u>People wash their hands for about 9 seconds. It, however, takes</u>

   <u>about 15 seconds to kill the germs.</u>

   _____

   _____

2. We have better health today than ever. People worry more about their health today.

   _____

   _____

   _____

C. Connect the sentences with *but* and *however*. Pay attention to punctuation (commas and periods).

1. Violent crime frightens us.
   We are more likely to die in a car.

   a.   _Violent crime frightens us, but we are more likely to die in a car._

   b.   _Violent crime frightens us. However, we are more likely to die in a car._

2. We like to watch violent TV shows.
   Violence makes us afraid.

   a. _____

   b. _____

3. I am more likely to die in a car accident.
   I fear an airplane crash more.

   a. _____

   b. _____

4. Women fear crime more than men.
   Crime happens more often to men.

   a. _____

   b. _____

5. Most crimes are not violent.
   The media focuses on unusual and violent crimes.

   a. _____

   b. _____

D. Finish the sentences.

1. Teenagers worry less than adults about dangers, but _____

   _____

2. Most spiders are not poisonous. However, _____

   _____

3. Many people are afraid of speaking in front of a group of people, but ___

_____

4. Jumping from an airplane is very scary. However, _____

_____

E. Find the mistakes in punctuation and capitalization. Correct the sentences.

1. Parents keep children inside for safety, however. These children often don't get enough exercise.

2. Cars are safer than ever however there are more accidents because people drive faster in safe cars.

3. Your chance of dying in an airplane is 1 in 7,178. But your chances of dying in a car accident is 1 in 98.

4. Adults worry too much about dangers. Teenagers however do not worry enough.

 F. Go online for more practice contrasting ideas with *however.*

Grammar | Comparative adjectives

We use **comparative adjectives** to compare two people, places, things, or ideas.

Crime is **high** in my neighborhood.   →   Crime is **higher** in yours.
I'm **afraid** of getting the flu.   →   My sister is **more afraid**.

Here are some rules to help you form comparative adjectives correctly.

- Add *-er* to one-syllable adjectives. (A *syllable* is a part of a word with a vowel sound. One-syllable words have one vowel sound.) Add *-r* when the adjective ends in *-e*.

  high → high**er**   late → late**r**

- When the one-syllable adjective ends in consonant + vowel + consonant, double the last consonant and add *-er*.

  big → bi**gger**   hot → ho**tter**

- Do not double the consonant when the adjective ends in *-w*, *-x*, or *-y*.

  low → low**er**   gray → gray**er**

- For two-syllable adjectives that end in -y, drop the -y and add -ier.

  scary → scar**ier**   crazy → craz**ier**

- For most other adjectives with two or more syllables, use *more* + adjective.

  fearful → **more** fearful   frightening → **more** frightening

- Use comparative adjective + *than* in sentences comparing two things.

  My neighborhood is **safer than** your neighborhood.
  Your neighborhood is **more dangerous than** my neighborhood.

Note: The words *good* and *bad* are irregular.

  good → **better**   bad → **worse**

A. Complete the chart with the comparative form of each adjective.

Adjective	Comparative Adjective
1. afraid	more afraid
2. big	
3. careful	
4. dangerous	
5. easy	
6. new	
7. reasonable	
8. safe	
9. smart	
10. violent	

B. Write sentences using the words and phrases. Use the comparative forms of the adjectives and *than*.

1. heart disease / mad cow disease / common

   Heart disease is more common than mad cow disease.

2. I believe / flying / driving / dangerous

   _____

3. I think / crime dramas / scary / real life

   _____

4. the crime rate in Canada in 2012 / the crime rate in Canada 20 years before / low

   _____

C. Go online for more practice with comparative adjectives.

D. Go online for the grammar expansion.

Unit Assignment   Write one or more paragraphs about an unreasonable fear

In this assignment, you are going to write one or more paragraphs about an unreasonable fear that you have or that you know about. Why is it unreasonable and how can you avoid the fear? As you prepare your paragraph(s), think about the Unit Question, "What are you afraid of?" Use information from Reading 1, Reading 2, the unit video, and your work in this unit to support your ideas. Refer to the Self-Assessment checklist on page 194.

Go to the Online Writing Tutor for a writing model and alternate Unit Assignments.

PLAN AND WRITE

A. BRAINSTORM Think of fears that you believe are unreasonable. Write four fears in the chart on page 193. Then tell why they are unreasonable.

Fear	Why It's Unreasonable
flying on an airplane	only 1 in 7,178 chance of dying in a plane crash

Critical Thinking **Tip**

Activity B helps you **develop** your ideas before you write. **Developing** your ideas lets you think them through and make them more complete. This will make your writing stronger.

B. **PLAN** Choose one fear from your chart in Activity A. Complete the activities.

1. Write a topic sentence. Use this sentence or write your own:

   _____ is an unreasonable fear because

   _____.

2. Explain the fear you chose and why you or people fear it.

3. Tell why it is unreasonable and how you can avoid that fear.

4. Write a concluding sentence.

C. **WRITE** Use your **PLAN** notes to write your paragraph(s). Go to *iQ Online* to use the Online Writing Tutor.

1. Write a topic sentence, supporting sentences, and a concluding sentence. Make sure you explain your fear and why it is unreasonable.

2. Look at the Self-Assessment checklist on page 194 to guide your writing.

REVISE AND EDIT

A. **PEER REVIEW** Read your partner's paragraph(s). Then go online and use the Peer Review worksheet. Discuss the review with your partner.

B. **REWRITE** Based on your partner's review, revise and rewrite your paragraph(s).

C. **EDIT** Complete the Self-Assessment checklist as you prepare to write the final draft of your paragraph(s). Be prepared to hand in your work or discuss it in class.

	SELF-ASSESSMENT
Yes **No**	
☐ ☐	Does your topic sentence introduce your topic and main idea?
☐ ☐	Do you use both opinions and facts in your supporting sentences?
☐ ☐	Does your concluding sentence remind readers of your main idea?
☐ ☐	Do you use *believe, think,* or *should* correctly to introduce opinions?
☐ ☐	Do you use comparative adjectives correctly?
☐ ☐	Does your paragraph include vocabulary words from the unit?
☐ ☐	Did you check your paragraph for correct punctuation especially in sentences with *however, but, because,* and *when*?
☐ ☐	Is the spelling correct? Check a dictionary if you are unsure.
☐ ☐	Did you check your grammar for correct use of verbs and infinitives?

 D. **REFLECT** Go to the Online Discussion Board to discuss these questions.

1. What is something new you learned in this unit?

2. Look back at the Unit Question—What are you afraid of? Is your answer different now than when you started the unit? If yes, how is it different? Why?

TRACK YOUR SUCCESS

Circle the words you have learned in this unit.

Nouns	Verbs	Adjectives
crime 🔑	affect 🔑 AWL	common 🔑
death 🔑	contain 🔑	negative 🔑 AWL
disease 🔑	frighten 🔑	reasonable 🔑
factor AWL	harm 🔑	scary 🔑
fat 🔑	report 🔑	violent 🔑
focus AWL		
pleasure 🔑		

🔑 Oxford 2000 keywords

AWL Academic Word List

Check (✓) the skills you learned. If you need more work on a skill, refer to the page(s) in parentheses.

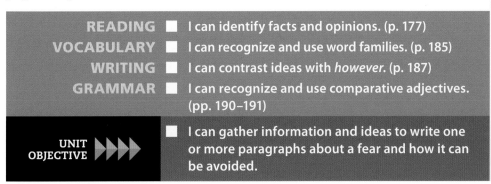

READING	☐ I can identify facts and opinions. (p. 177)
VOCABULARY	☐ I can recognize and use word families. (p. 185)
WRITING	☐ I can contrast ideas with *however*. (p. 187)
GRAMMAR	☐ I can recognize and use comparative adjectives. (pp. 190–191)
UNIT OBJECTIVE ▶▶▶▶	☐ I can gather information and ideas to write one or more paragraphs about a fear and how it can be avoided.

AUTHORS AND CONSULTANTS

Author

Sarah Lynn holds an M.A. in TESOL from Teachers College, Columbia University. She has taught English to speakers of other languages for over twenty-five years, both in the U.S. and abroad, and currently teaches at the Harvard Bridge Program in Cambridge, MA. As a teacher trainer, Ms. Lynn has led workshops on the multilevel classroom, learner persistence, reading strategies and skills, writing in low-level classes, and self-directed learning. Ms. Lynn has also written numerous teacher resource books and student textbooks for English Language Learners.

Series Consultants

ONLINE INTEGRATION

Chantal Hemmi holds an Ed.D. TEFL and is a Japan-based teacher trainer and curriculum designer. Since leaving her position as Academic Director of the British Council in Tokyo, she has been teaching at the Center for Language Education and Research at Sophia University on an EAP/CLIL program offered for undergraduates. She delivers lectures and teacher trainings throughout Japan, Indonesia, and Malaysia.

COMMUNICATIVE GRAMMAR

Nancy Schoenfeld holds an M.A. in TESOL from Biola University in La Mirada, California, and has been an English language instructor since 2000. She has taught ESL in California and Hawaii and EFL in Thailand and Kuwait. She has also trained teachers in the United States and Indonesia. Her interests include teaching vocabulary, extensive reading, and student motivation. She is currently an English Language Instructor at Kuwait University.

WRITING

Marguerite Ann Snow holds a Ph.D. in Applied Linguistics from UCLA. She teaches in the TESOL M.A. program in the Charter College of Education at California State University, Los Angeles. She was a Fulbright scholar in Hong Kong and Cyprus. In 2006, she received the President's Distinguished Professor award at Cal State, LA. She has trained EFL teachers in Algeria, Argentina, Brazil, Egypt, Libya, Morocco, Pakistan, Peru, Spain, and Turkey. She is the author/editor of publications in the areas of integrated content, English for academic purposes, and standards for English teaching and learning. She recently served as a co-editor of *Teaching English as a Second or Foreign Language* (4th ed.).

VOCABULARY

Cheryl Boyd Zimmerman is a Professor at California State University, Fullerton. She specializes in second-language vocabulary acquisition, an area in which she is widely published. She teaches graduate courses on second-language acquisition, culture, vocabulary, and the fundamentals of TESOL and is a frequent invited speaker on topics related to vocabulary teaching and learning. She is the author of *Word Knowledge: A Vocabulary Teacher's Handbook* and Series Director of *Inside Reading, Inside Writing,* and *Inside Listening and Speaking,* all published by Oxford University Press.

ASSESSMENT

Lawrence J. Zwier holds an M.A. in TESL from the University of Minnesota. He is currently the Associate Director for Curriculum Development at the English Language Center at Michigan State University in East Lansing. He has taught ESL/EFL in the United States, Saudi Arabia, Malaysia, Japan, and Singapore.

iQ ONLINE extends your learning beyond the classroom. This online content is specifically designed for you! *iQ Online* gives you flexible access to essential content.

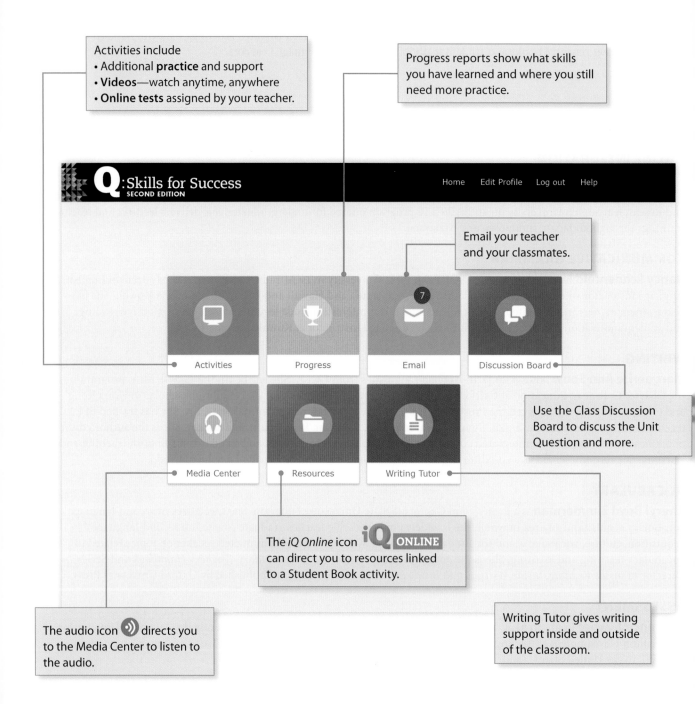

Activities include
• Additional **practice** and support
• **Videos**—watch anytime, anywhere
• **Online tests** assigned by your teacher.

Progress reports show what skills you have learned and where you still need more practice.

Email your teacher and your classmates.

Use the Class Discussion Board to discuss the Unit Question and more.

The *iQ Online* icon can direct you to resources linked to a Student Book activity.

The audio icon directs you to the Media Center to listen to the audio.

Writing Tutor gives writing support inside and outside of the classroom.

SEE THE INSIDE FRONT COVER FOR HOW TO REGISTER FOR *iQ ONLINE* FOR THE FIRST TIME.

Take Control of Your Learning

You have the choice of where and how you complete the activities. Access your activities and view your progress at any time.

Your teacher may

- assign *iQ Online* as homework,
- do the activities with you in class, or
- let you complete the activities at a pace that is right for you.

iQ Online makes it easy to access everything you need.

Set Clear Goals

STEP 1 If it is your first time, look through the site. See what learning opportunities are available.

STEP 2 The Student Book provides the framework and purpose for each online activity. Before going online, notice the goal of the exercises you are going to do.

STEP 3 Stay on top of your work, following the teacher's instructions.

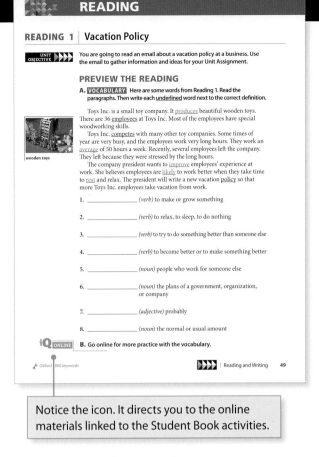

> Notice the icon. It directs you to the online materials linked to the Student Book activities.

STEP 4 Use *iQ Online* for review. You can use the materials any time. It is easy for you to do follow-up activities when you have missed a class or want to review.

Manage Your Progress

The activities in *iQ Online* are designed for you to work independently. You can become a confident learner by monitoring your progress and reviewing the activities at your own pace. You may already be used to working online, but if you are not, go to your teacher for guidance.

Check 'View Reports' to monitor your progress. The reports let you track your own progress at a glance. Think about your own performance and set new goals that are right for you, following the teacher's instructions.

iQ Online is a research-based solution specifically designed for English language learners that extends learning beyond the classroom. I hope these steps help you make the most of this essential content.

C. n. Hemm

Chantal Hemmi, EdD TEFL
Center for Language Education and Research
Sophia University, Japan

🔊 Q: *Skills for Success Second Edition* audio can be found in the Media Center.

Follow these steps:

Step 1: Go to iQOnlinePractice.com.

Step 2: Click on the Media Center icon. 🎧

Step 3: Choose to stream or download ⬇ the audio file you select. Not all audio files are available for download.

Class Audio

Unit	Page	Listen	Download
Unit 1			
1	3	The Q Classroom	⬇
1	6	Work With the Reading	⬇
1	13	Work With the Reading	⬇
Unit 2			
2	28	The Q Classroom	⬇
2	32	Work With the Reading	⬇
2	38	Work With the Reading	⬇
Unit 3			
3	55	The Q Classroom	⬇
3	58	Work With the Reading	⬇
3	65	Work With the Reading	

Back

Unit	Activity	Track File Name
Unit 1	The Q Classroom, p. 2	Q2e_01_RW_U01_ Q_Classroom.mp3
	Work With the Reading, p. 6	Q2e_01_RW_U01_ Reading1.mp3
	Work With the Reading, p. 11	Q2e_01_RW_U01_Reading2.mp3
Unit 2	The Q Classroom, p. 25	Q2e_01_RW_U02_Q_Classroom.mp3
	Work With the Reading, p. 28	Q2e_01_RW_U02_Reading1.mp3
	Work With the Reading, p. 34	Q2e_01_RW_U02_Reading2.mp3
Unit 3	The Q Classroom, p. 46	Q2e_01_RW_U03_Q_Classroom.mp3
	Work With the Reading, p. 50	Q2e_01_RW_U03_Reading1.mp3
	Work With the Reading, p. 58	Q2e_01_RW_U03_Reading2.mp3
Unit 4	The Q Classroom, p. 73	Q2e_01_RW_U04_Q_Classroom.mp3
	Work With the Reading, p. 76	Q2e_01_RW_U04_Reading1.mp3
	Work With the Reading, p. 82	Q2e_01_RW_U04_Reading2.mp3
Unit 5	The Q Classroom, p. 97	Q2e_01_RW_U05_Q_Classroom.mp3
	Work With the Reading, p. 100	Q2e_01_RW_U05_Reading1.mp3
	Work With the Reading, p. 107	Q2e_01_RW_U05_Reading2.mp3
Unit 6	The Q Classroom, p. 120	Q2e_01_RW_U06_Q_Classroom.mp3
	Work With the Reading, p. 124	Q2e_01_RW_U06_Reading1.mp3
	Work With the Reading, p. 131	Q2e_01_RW_U06_Reading2.mp3
Unit 7	The Q Classroom, p. 146	Q2e_01_RW_U07_Q_Classroom.mp3
	Work With the Reading, p. 151	Q2e_01_RW_U07_Reading1.mp3
	Work With the Reading, p. 156	Q2e_01_RW_U07_Reading2.mp3
Unit 8	The Q Classroom, p. 171	Q2e_01_RW_U08_Q_Classroom.mp3
	Work With the Reading, p. 174	Q2e_01_RW_U08_Reading1.mp3
	Work With the Reading, p. 181	Q2e_01_RW_U08_Reading2.mp3

VOCABULARY LIST AND CEFR CORRELATION

🔑 The keywords of the **Oxford 2000** have been carefully selected by a group of language experts and experienced teachers as the words which should receive priority in vocabulary study because of their importance and usefulness.

AWL The Academic Word List is the most principled and widely accepted list of academic words. Averil Coxhead gathered information from academic materials across the academic disciplines to create this word list.

The Common European Framework of Reference for Languages (CEFR) provides a basic description of what language learners have to do to use language effectively. The system contains 6 reference levels: **A1, A2, B1, B2, C1, C2.** CEFR leveling provided by the Word Family Framework, created by Richard West and published by the British Council. http://www.learnenglish.org.uk/wff/

UNIT 1

career (n.) 🔑, A1
company (n.) 🔑, A1
creative (adj.) AWL, B1
customer (n.) 🔑, A1
decision (n.) 🔑, A1
event (n.) 🔑, A1
flexible (adj.) AWL, B1
match (v.) 🔑, A2
plan (v.) (n.) 🔑, A1
product (n.) 🔑, A1
regular (adj.) 🔑, A1
result (n.) 🔑, A1
skill (n.) 🔑, A1
solve (v.) 🔑, A2
success (n.) 🔑, A1

UNIT 2

celebrate (v.) 🔑, A2
community (n.) 🔑 AWL, A1
international (adj.) 🔑, A1
lonely (adj.) 🔑, B1
market (n.) 🔑, A1
million (no.) 🔑, A1
neighborhood (n.), B1
opportunity (n.) 🔑, A1
own (adj.) 🔑, A1
population (n.), A1

several (adj.) 🔑, A1
sights (n.) 🔑, B1
support (v.) 🔑, B2

UNIT 3

abroad (adj.) 🔑, B1
attitude (n.) 🔑 AWL, A1
average (n.) 🔑, A2
benefit (n.) 🔑 AWL, A1
compete (v.), A2
connect (v.) 🔑, B1
discover (v.) 🔑, A1
employee (n.), A1
improve (v.) 🔑, A1
likely (adv.) 🔑, A1
policy (n.) AWL, A1
positive (adj.) 🔑 AWL, A1
produce (v.) 🔑, A1
reduce (v.) 🔑, A1
rest (v.) 🔑, A2

UNIT 4

breathe (v.) 🔑, A2
concentrate (v.) 🔑 AWL, A2
distracted (adj.), B2
effect (n.) 🔑, A1
embarrassed (adj.) 🔑, B1
honest (adj.) 🔑, B1

increase (v.) 🔑, A1
natural (adj.) 🔑, A1
nervous (adj.) 🔑, B1
pretend (v.) 🔑, B2
prevent (v.) 🔑, B1
protect (v.) 🔑, B1
rate (n.) 🔑, A2
surprise (v.) 🔑, B1

UNIT 5

association (n.), A2
according to (prep.) 🔑, A1
disorganized (adj.), B2
exciting (adj.) 🔑, B1
familiar (adj.) 🔑, A1
fan (n.), A2
fit (v.) 🔑, A1
form (v.) 🔑, A1
history (n.) 🔑, A1
invent (v.) 🔑, B1
kick (v.) 🔑, A2
notice (v.) 🔑, B1
popular (adj.) 🔑, A2
similar (adj.) 🔑 AWL, A1
tie (n.) 🔑, B2
volume (n.) 🔑 AWL, A2

UNIT 6

admit *(v.)* 🔑, A1
avoid *(v.)* 🔑, A1
behave *(v.)* 🔑, B1
boss *(n.)* 🔑, A2
fire *(v.)* 🔑, B1
furniture *(n.)* 🔑, B1
opinion *(n.)* 🔑, A1
practice *(v.)* 🔑, A2
punishment *(n.)* 🔑, B1
purpose *(n.)* 🔑, A2
relationship *(n.)* 🔑, B1
reputation *(n.)*, B1
require *(v.)* 🔑 AWL, A1
respect *(v.)* 🔑, B1
trouble *(n.)* 🔑, A1
trust *(v.)* 🔑, A2

UNIT 7

century *(n.)* 🔑, A1
ceremony *(n.)* 🔑, B1
collect *(v.)* 🔑, A2
define *(v.)* AWL, A1
dive *(v.)*, B1
grown *(adj.)* 🔑, B2
judgment *(n.)* 🔑, A2
legal *(adj.)* 🔑 AWL, A1
organize *(v.)* 🔑, A2
participate *(v.)* AWL, B1
permission *(n.)* 🔑, B1
represent *(v.)* 🔑, B1
responsibility *(n.)* 🔑, B1
right *(v.)* 🔑, B1
tie *(v.)* 🔑, A2
village *(n.)* 🔑, A1
vote *(v.)* 🔑, A2

UNIT 8

affect *(v.)* 🔑 AWL, A1
common *(adj.)* 🔑, A1
contain *(v.)* 🔑, A1
crime *(n.)* 🔑, A2
death *(n.)* 🔑, A1
disease *(n.)* 🔑, A1
factor *(n.)* AWL, B1
fat *(n.)* 🔑, B1
focus *(n.)* AWL, A2
frighten *(v.)* 🔑, B1
harm *(v.)* 🔑, B2
negative *(adj.)* 🔑 AWL, A2
pleasure *(n.)* 🔑, A2
reasonable *(adj.)* 🔑, A2
report *(v.)* 🔑, A2
scary *(adj.)* 🔑, B1
violent *(adj.)* 🔑, B1